A BOY'S
SHORT LIFE

Anna Haebich is a multi-aw nd
historian, who is especially re search and work
with Aboriginal communities and in particular the Noongar
people. She is part of a large Noongar family through marriage.
Her career combines university teaching, research, curatorship,
creative writing and visual arts. Her publications include *Broken
Circles: Fragmenting Indigenous Families 1800–2000*, which is the first
and most comprehensive national history of Australia's Stolen
Generations; the definitive history *For Their Own Good: Aborigines
and Government in the South West of Western Australia 1900–1940*; and
Spinning the Dream: Assimilation in Australia. Anna is a John Curtin
Distinguished Professor at Curtin University. She is currently
researching Aboriginal performing arts in Western Australia, past
and present.

Steve Mickler is Head of the School of Media, Culture and
Creative Arts at Curtin University. He has a diverse background
in Indigenous affairs and academia, having previously worked in
Aboriginal Affairs in the Northern Territory and Western Australia,
including in the public affairs sections of the Department of
Aboriginal Affairs, ATSIC and as a research officer with the Royal
Commission into Aboriginal Deaths in Custody. His previous
publications include *Gambling on the First Race: A Comment on
Racism and Talkback Radio, The Myth of Privilege: Aboriginal Status,
Media Visions, Public Ideas* and numerous journal articles dealing
with media and public representation of Indigenous affairs.

Also published by
UWA Publishing
for the Charles and Joy Staples South
West Region Publications Fund:

*For Their Own Good: Aborigines and
Government in the South West of Western
Australia 1900–1940*
Anna Haebich

The South West from Dawn till Dusk
Rob Olver

*Contested Country: A History of the
Northcliffe area, Western Australia*
Patricia and Ian Crawford

*Richard Spencer: Napoleonic War Naval
Hero and Australian Pioneer*
Gwen Chessell

A Story to Tell
Laurel Nannup

*Alexander Collie: Colonial Surgeon,
Naturalist and Explorer*
Gwen Chessell

*Shaking Hands on the Fringe: Negotiating the
Aboriginal World at King George's Sound*
Tiffany Shellam

*"It's Still in my Heart, This is my Country":
The Single Noongar Claim History*, South
West Aboriginal Land and Sea Council,
John Host with Chris Owen

Mamang
An old story retold by Kim Scott, Iris
Woods and the Wirlomin Noongar
Language and Stories Project, with
artwork by Jeffrey Farmer, Helen Nelly
and Roma Winmar (Yibiyung)

Noongar Mambara Bakitj
An old story retold by Kim Scott, Lomas
Roberts and the Wirlomin Noongar
Language and Stories Project, with
artwork by Geoffrey Woods and
Anthony Roberts

Guy Grey-Smith: Life Force
Andrew Gaynor

Dwoort Baal Kaat
An old story retold by Kim Scott,
Russell Nelly and the Wirlomin
Noongar Language and Stories Project,
with artwork by Helen (Ing) Hall

Yira Boornak Nyininy
An old story retold by Kim Scott,
Hazel Brown, Roma Winmar and
the Wirlomin Noongar Language
and Stories Project, with artwork by
Anthony (Troy) Roberts

*Fire and Hearth: A study of Aboriginal usage
and European usurpation in south-western
Australia*
Sylvia J. Hallam

The Charles and Joy Staples South
West Region Publications Fund was
established in 1984 on the basis of a
generous donation to The University
of Western Australia by Charles and
Joy Staples.

The purpose of the Fund was to
make the results of research on the
South West region of Western Australia
widely available so as to assist the people
of the South West region and those in
government and private organisations
concerned with South West projects to
appreciate the needs and possibilities
of the region in the widest possible
historical perspective.

The Fund is administered by a
committee whose aims are to make
possible the publication (either by full
or part funding), by UWA Publishing,
of research in any discipline relevant
to the South West region.

A BOY'S SHORT LIFE

The story of
Warren Braedon/Louis Johnson

Anna Haebich and
Steve Mickler

U W
A P
UWA PUBLISHING

First published in 2000 by Fremantle Arts Centre Press as 'A Boy's Short Life' in
Broken Circles: Fragmenting Indigenous Families 1800–2000 by Anna Haebich.

This revised edition published in 2013 by UWA Publishing
Crawley, Western Australia 6009
www.uwap.uwa.edu.au
for the Charles and Joy Staples
South West Region Publications Fund

THE UNIVERSITY OF
WESTERN AUSTRALIA
Achieve International Excellence

National Library of Australia
Cataloguing-in-Publication data:

A boy's short life : the story of Warren Braedon / Louis Johnson / Anna
Haebich and Steve Mickler.

9781742585079 (pbk.)
Includes bibliographical references.

Johnson, Louis St John.
Adopted children—Australia—Biography.
Children, Aboriginal Australian—Biography

362.734

Cover photograph of Louis Johnson courtesy of the Johnson family.
Internal photographs courtesy of the Johnson family.
Typeset by J & M Typesetting
Printed by Lightning Source

Contents

We have made a number of editorial revisions to the original text, largely for the purposes of enhancing clarity and greater concision for the benefit of a contemporary young readership. We have also made stylistic changes to some terminology, however, the narrative structure is unchanged from the original.

It is our hope that *A Boy's Short Life* in this new publication format will continue to make a meaningful contribution to understanding the social catastrophe that engulfed the Indigenous peoples of Australia.

Anna Haebich and Steve Mickler
June 2013

Synopsis

This book is an account of the life and tragic death of a young Aboriginal man, Louis St John Johnson, who was born Warren Braedon. He was one of the Stolen Generations – the tens of thousands of infants and children who were removed from their families and communities and placed in foster homes, state and church institutions or put up for adoption under various state and federal government policies throughout the twentieth century.

Louis was born in 1973, a year after Aboriginal activists famously protested against the national myth, 'terra nullius' – that Australia belonged to no one before the British arrived in 1788 – by setting up a tent embassy on the grounds of the national parliament in Canberra. He died in 1992 at the hands of murderers, the same year the Australian High Court recognised that Aboriginal people held native title over their traditional homelands.

Colonialism

Alice Springs and its surrounds have a turbulent history of colonisation and of ongoing conflicts and readjustments between incoming settlers and resident Aboriginal people. The town had its origins in the establishment of a telegraph station in 1871. Called Stuart until 1933, the tiny outpost served local pastoral stations. From the beginning there was conflict with the Arrernte, Luritja and Warlpiri peoples whose country was being colonised. Their hunting and gathering economy was increasingly marginalised by the pastoral economy and land acquisitions that dispossessed them. Backed by police and the Native Patrol Force, the settlers inflicted serious casualties and an estimated 500 to 1000 Aboriginal people were killed during the first three decades of white settlement.[1]

To survive, Aboriginal people were obliged to comply over a long period of time with harsh government measures of pacification and population control. These included food rationing at pastoral, mining and telegraph stations, and relocation to reserved areas and missions.[2] In these 'sanctuaries' Aboriginal people could at least hope to stay alive. Various areas of economic and social interdependency also developed. Aboriginal men and women became essential to the pastoral industry and hence the whole regional economy.[3] They also worked in mining, domestic service and mission industries. Tim Rowse describes a strategy of welfare colonialism that sought to cut links between the generations by separating Aboriginal children from their families in dormitories on missions and government settlements, a practice that accelerated following the Second World War.[4] The town of Stuart became a centre where Aboriginal people could get work, rations and medical treatment. Many simply had nowhere else to go. However, their presence created tensions with townsfolk, many of whom relied on their menial labour but resented their presence in town. Settler efforts to control them clashed with the Aboriginal people's determination to maintain their own ways of living that combined elements of traditional Aboriginal and European lifestyles.

Federal government control of Aboriginal people in the Northern Territory began in 1911 and was manifested in the *Aboriginals Ordinance 1918*. Its harsh clauses embodied segregation and control under the guise of a policy of protection, implemented through restrictions on Aboriginal employment, mobility and family and personal matters. The Ordinance was enforced locally by police officers who also issued welfare in the form of rations. The continuing influence of nineteenth century Social Darwinist assumptions was evident in the Aboriginals Department's guiding belief that little could be done to save 'full-bloods' from 'extinction' apart from issuing rations to 'smooth the dying pillow'.[5] By contrast, the Department acted purposefully to limit the growing 'half-caste' population through strict controls over the women's sexual contacts. It also removed and institutionalised their children. The Bungalow, opened in Stuart in 1914, acted as a government depot for some 'half-caste' children of Aboriginal women and mining and pastoral workers in Central Australia. Consisting of a few old iron huts next to the police station and the hotel, the original Bungalow housed up to sixty children at a time during the 1920s. After basic schooling the children were sent out to work, under police control, as domestics, labourers and pastoral workers. Living conditions were deplorable and, despite exposés by the press in the southern states, continued virtually unchanged until the Bungalow was eventually relocated to the site of the Old Telegraph Station in 1932.

Assimilation

National attention was focused on the region following reports of a punitive police massacre of approximately one hundred Warlpiri men, women and children at Coniston Station in 1928. Locally there was more alarm about the growing 'half-caste' problem. The Chief Protector of Aborigines, Dr Cecil Cook (appointed in 1927), embraced the eugenicist policy of biological absorption, aimed at breeding out the 'mixed race' altogether, although federal authorities endeavoured to limit Cook's enthusiasm. Influenced by anthropologist A. P. Elkin, the *Aboriginals Ordinance 1939* introduced the new policy of social assimilation that promised to bring full citizenship and improved living conditions for all Aboriginal people. Tribal and semi-detribalised people were to be protected in special settlements that would, over generations, in the words of the Federal Minister for the Interior, John McEwan, 'transform these people from a nomadic tribal state to take their place in a civilised community'.[1] Removal of children of mixed descent would continue as a focus of assimilation policy as the Northern Territory Administrator explained in 1952:

> Those most easily assimilated are persons of mixed blood, provided that they are able to enjoy from an early and impressionable age the medical care, training, teaching and general living conditions available to the community at large.[2]

With the exception of a small number of children of legally married 'half-castes' who could remain with their parents unless they were deemed 'neglected', 'half-caste' children in the Northern Territory faced the very real prospect of being permanently removed from their families.

The *Welfare Ordinance 1953* was an attempt to introduce a welfare model for all, regardless of race. In fact it maintained separate treatment of all categories of people of Aboriginal descent and reinforced gradations of racial descent and observance of strict caste barriers existing in Alice Springs at the time. This exacerbated racial tensions in the town. For seventy years Alice Springs had remained small, having only 400 white residents by the Second World War. The war had boosted this number to 6000 – for the first time outnumbering Aboriginal people. This shift from the enforced interdependence of a small frontier population was accompanied by a growing sensitivity to matters of race. A study of social relationships in Alice Springs in the mid-1940s found that the 'mixed race' population of 300, many of them graduates of the Bungalow, tended to stick together, to marry each other and to see themselves as a distinct group within the town.[3] Aboriginal people of 'mixed descent' no longer came under special welfare legislation. They were to be assimilated into white Australian society. This isolated them from their 'full-blood' kin at the same time as it endeavoured to force them into a society that did not accept them as equals. In Alice Springs they were pressured by government officials to move into austere cottages at the Gap on the outskirts of town. They were to dissociate themselves from their Aboriginal relatives in the camps who were directed to settle in the vicinity of the Bungalow.[4] Despite stated intentions to assimilate 'mixed race' families into the wider Australian community, the administration persisted in treating them as a distinct group requiring special supervision and control. Their households were subject to surveillance by Welfare Branch officers in their quest to transform them into nuclear families. Mothers and children were the focus of their attention and the officers carried with them:

> ...diaries in which they recorded salient notes on their clients' domestic habits. If a woman began to leave her children unattended, drink heavily, neglect the washing, or otherwise fail in her duties, the welfare officers warned her. After several warnings, the Welfare Branch would take the derelict family to court.[5]

The Welfare Branch could intervene more directly by simply taking children who 'lived in remote areas or homes that were otherwise considered unsuitable' and placing them in institutions.[6]

Aboriginal people of 'full descent' were declared to be 'wards' under the Ordinance. This ostensibly non-race specific category was used in practice to continue regulating Aboriginal people's lifestyles, ability to manage their own affairs, standards of behaviour and personal associations. The stated intention was to assist them to make the transition from traditional to 'assimilated' life.[7] Police and Welfare Branch patrol officers, appointed from the mid-1940s, regulated their movement and residency through removal to reserves and government and mission settlements, enforced their exclusion from areas prohibited to unemployed Aboriginal people, and removed their camps from the vicinity of towns.

In Alice Springs controlling the movement and residency of 'full-blood' people was a constant theme of local town development. As was evident in the case of the famous Arrernte painter Albert Namatjira, this control was invariably exerted to suit white prerogatives. During the 1950s Namatjira purchased a block of land in the town, but was refused permission to build a house on it because it was assumed that his family would cause trouble and the value of adjacent properties would fall. This theme continued through into the 1960s. The major settlement at the Bungalow, with 300 residents, was closed to make way for tourism interests in 1961. The people were relocated to a new government settlement, Amoonguna, fourteen kilometres southeast of the town.

Established in 1960, Amoonguna was to become a self-contained village for residents and visiting Aboriginal people. Rationalised as a training ground and conceived by the government as producing assimilated citizens who could live in houses and aspire to permanent work and a settled, urban life, the populating of Amoonguna relied on the fact that food ration distribution was concentrated there. A place beset with internal strife and resembling more the environment of a refugee camp than the ideal 'white Australian lifestyle', the settlement proved a failure by the end of the decade as people moved off to sites closer to town once better wages, pensions and other social security payments became available. In any case, these 'assimilation' projects failed because people rejected the authoritarian regime that endeavoured to enforce institutional housing and living patterns, to prevent the use of alcohol, and to break the strength of residents' adherence to kinship structures, traditions of free movement and ties to the country. The Welfare Branch's 1969 annual report commented:

> Detribalisation in the sense of surrender of the basic social organisation and social arrangements has not ... gone very far, and traditional institutions such as marriage patterns, and traditional attachment to particular geographical areas are still greatly respected.[8]

Civil rights

The year 1964 marked the beginning of the period of dramatic change and upheaval for Aboriginal people in the Alice Springs region that continued into the 1970s. The change began as the 1953 Ordinance gave way to the *Social Welfare Ordinance 1964*, which finally removed all legal controls based on Aboriginality. The phasing out of this restrictive legislation, and its special measures of welfare and control, that included the lifting of restrictions on Aboriginal access to alcohol, was cognate with the granting of Aboriginal people's right to vote in federal elections in 1962 and the introduction of award wages for Aboriginal pastoral workers in 1968. However, as Aboriginal historian Barbara Cummings explains, these legal advances were circumscribed since the 1964 ordinance, and continued to be directed punitively at Aboriginal people. While officially aimed at a wider range of persons 'the mechanics of [its] language' were derived from the earlier, repealed legislation so that, although bureaucrats were required to deal with people on the basis of need rather than 'race', the legislation continued to be applied mainly to Aboriginal people. The welfare administration had also retained most of the same personnel, practices, values and rationalities of the assimilationist era and its determination to control Aboriginal people.[1]

Conditions for Aboriginal families in Alice Springs were also changing. Earning a living in town had always been a precarious business: from the 1930s, at least, some town families had earned small cash wages by doing odd jobs, working on the town sanitary carts or doing seasonal work on the nearby stations. Pressures on the small pool of labour increased as pastoralists in the region sacked Aboriginal workers following the introduction of award wages and mechanisation of the industry. Families were forced to move into Alice Springs to find work and a place to camp. Some relief came from the inflow of cash from federal social security benefits gradually extended to Aboriginal people from the 1960s. With families 'liberated' from rationing and with the major reforms in social welfare legislation in 1964, the government's strict controls over Aboriginal people in town camps and on its missions and settlements came to an end. This made it more difficult for government authorities to monitor the presence of Aboriginal people in Alice Springs. This also created new problems of adjustment for Aboriginal people.

Equality in name only

Tensions with white residents flared as overcrowding and disorder in the camps increased. They openly attacked the government's actions to remove controls over Aboriginal people's movement and access to alcohol and social security benefits. Articles in the Alice Springs newspaper the *Centralian Advocate* summarised here give an idea of the public representation of disorder amongst Aboriginal people at the time, a state that was simplistically attributed to the granting of drinking rights:

> Fifty-eight Aboriginal people charged with drunkenness are kept in jail an extra twenty-four hours awaiting the arrival of the magistrate.[1]

> Of sixty-seven court cases on Christmas Eve, fifty were for Aboriginal drunkenness.[2]

> Aborigines reported fighting on Todd Street.[3]

Reports of continued brawls involving Aborigines in Alice Springs streets, camps and hotels.[4]

Police are attacked by Aborigines with rocks at the Alice Springs Show after they arrest a group of Aborigines for drunkenness.[5]

An Aboriginal man assaults a barmaid who refused to serve him beer in an Alice Springs hotel.[6]

A drunken Aboriginal man is sentenced to fourteen days hard labour for stabbing another Aboriginal man.[7]

That many of these events related to intra-communal violence suggests an actual breakdown in internal Aboriginal social control mechanisms.

The further development of Alice Springs also contributed to deteriorating conditions for Aboriginal people. By the 1970s the Alice Springs population had reached 10,000 and this rapid residential growth saw the introduction of new facilities and services, such as a drive-in theatre, ABC television, a commercial radio station, a swimming pool, hospital upgrading and a new high school. These developments affected established relationships between Aboriginal people and whites in several ways. As land was increasingly taken over for residential purposes and its value grew Aboriginal people were pressured by local authorities to move away from town or were squeezed into ever-more concentrated areas. Tourism's interest in presenting Alice Springs as a safe and clean holiday destination added to the pressure to remove Aboriginal camps.

This was a familiar scenario of marginalising Indigenous campers in country towns such as Broome and Cairns where tourism had no place for residents who did not benefit the town in some way. The touristic attractions of art, craft and corroborees aside, town camps were deemed undesirable. The pressure to reduce the number of camps struck against Aboriginal traditions of distinct groups, based on geographic and linguistic affiliation, living largely independently of one another. No doubt Aboriginal people also resented their exclusion from enjoying the benefits of the new facilities and services brought by development. Camp residents had specific ways of organising and relating both externally and internally. They camped in locations that were roughly aligned to their homelands; for example, people from areas south of the town would camp on its southern side. Moreover, the town, being the regional centre, meant that many were visitors for the purposes of medical treatment, holidays from pastoral work, court appearances, shopping and visiting relations. As Jeff Collman points out camping arrangements were strategic for resisting outside interference, an important matter given the continuing government practice of removing children from conditions of apparent neglect.[8] A report by the Central Australian Aboriginal Congress (CAAC) described conditions in 1976:

> The majority of these people live in grossly overcrowded and sub-standard housing and few have even the barest facilities such as toilets. There is a large number of unemployed men not receiving any benefits and obviously the only method of survival is by sharing the limited income from pensions

The paper went on to explain:

> The situation is due to in part 'deplorable conditions' of Aboriginal people living in the open in the riverbeds adjacent to town. While the creekbeds are said to be the traditional home of these people it was no excuse for allowing people black or white to camp indiscriminately in a town area.[14]

The early 1970s – the time of Warren Braedon's birth and removal from his mother Dawna – marked the climax of a period of serious conflict and neglectful treatment of Aboriginal people in Alice Springs. Old ways of government repression, police control and bullying of camp town residents were no longer viable and mainstream welfare services were unable to cope with the scale of Aboriginal need. The Aboriginal population in town increased over the decade from between 200 and 500 to just under 1000. The influx into the town camps, new Aboriginal citizenship rights and the inflow of cash benefits to replace rations were all contributing to a new order. Still town residents called on the same old repressive remedies to restore law and order: imprisonment, harassment of town campers, and removal of children from their families. Racial tensions peaked following federal government intervention to establish Aboriginal controlled organisations in the town that began to shift local power relations between white and black. Tragically this positive initiative was too late to save Warren Braedon from his fate.

The flooding of the town's court with people charged with drunkenness became a daily routine. David Parsons, a lawyer with the Central Australian Aboriginal Legal Aid Service, recalled his first impressions in early 1974:

> I walked past this line of Aboriginal people as I was on my way to court ... assuming that everyone was lining up for an injection outside something like the Health Department, and I looked at the next building, assuming I'd got the wrong building, and no, it must have been the court house. So I walked back again and sure enough, it was the morning's list. There were 127 people, most of whom were charged with drunkenness.[15]

Many people ended up in gaol. In 1973 the federal government moved to have public drunkenness decriminalised and this was implemented in July the following year. But it was not long before townsfolk demanded the reintroduction of drunkenness as an offence, arguing there had been a further breakdown in law and order.[16]

The perilous health of Aboriginal people, particularly infants, came under the spotlight. Their drastic social circumstances are perhaps no better indicated than in the fact that Central Australia in the 1960s reportedly had the highest infant mortality rate in the world – one in four Aboriginal infants died.[17] At the same time the birth rate in the predominantly Aboriginal population in the Territory was 33.3 per cent – compared with the national average of 20 per cent.[18] Indeed there appeared to be a crisis in Aboriginal parenting. F. Thornton notes that the primary responsibility for child-care fell on Aboriginal women:

In both the traditional and the semi-traditional ways, the women are the ones responsible for the children and for the family's welfare, arranging for shelter, food, placement of children whose parents have died or are unable to care for them for short or long periods ... Many women in the fringe camps and in households in the town area, are burdened with very heavy tribal and family responsibilities and are receiving little support.[19]

That many Aboriginal women in the early 1970s were finding it difficult to meet these demands is suggested by the reports of drinking and violence in the camps referred to above and the high rates of hospitalisation of children and infants.[20] While most town residents continued to blame the parents' consumption of alcohol and bad behaviour local missionaries pointed to the desperate need for special accommodation and assistance for mothers with sick children and facilities to train mothers in hygiene and the proper care of children who had been hospitalised.[21] In January 1973, the month Warren Braedon was born, the Federal Minister for Aboriginal Affairs, Gordon Bryant, threatened to sack public servants if 'something was not done about Aboriginal infant mortality'.[22]

Self-determination and backlash

In 1972 the new federal Labor government had set up the Department of Aboriginal Affairs and, following the adoption of the policy of self-determination, supported Aboriginal communities to establish self-managed organisations that were incorporated under federal legislation. These organisations, initially involved in health, legal aid, community government and land matters, were mainly funded by federal grants. New corporations established in Alice Springs in 1973 were the Central Australian Aboriginal Congress (CAAC), the Central Land Council, and the Central Australian Aboriginal Legal Aid Service (CAALAS). These organisations significantly increased the capacity for Aboriginal people to negotiate change and development, to put funding agencies and mainstream welfare institutions at one remove, and to have more control over processes and decisions affecting them. Pat Miller, the director of Aboriginal Legal Aid in 1993, and whose father was a founder of the organisation, describes this outcome:

> The incorporation came through in 1973. Then they went about employing a lawyer, and it just sort of flowed from there, it just grew and grew and grew. As the demand grew, more and more people became aware of their rights, so right up to today people walk in the door demanding legal assistance and advice because they've come across injustice just across the street or out on a station, things like that.[1]

The Central Land Council began the work of organising the traditional landowners to make their claims under the Northern Territory *Aboriginal Land Rights Act 1976* and over the next two decades lands were progressively returned to owners in Central Australia. In the town, fourteen Aboriginal areas and campsites were granted leases by 1979, which provided security and enabled houses and ablution facilities to be built on them. Not surprisingly many white residents felt threatened by this newfound power and labelled workers in organisations like CAALAS as 'radicals and southern stirrers' who were interfering in local customs and upsetting Aboriginal people. They resented the town's growing reputation in the national and international media as a 'particularly troublesome place with regard to race relations'.[2] The Northern Territory government was also antagonistic to the federal Labor government's local interventions that were seen to conflict with their own push for full self-government. A further factor contributing to high racial tensions was that race had 'a long tradition in the Northern Territory whereby whites use

Aborigines and their alleged problems as political resources in their own struggles for local power'.[3] Discrimination and exploitation were entrenched in the town's public institutions, services and general attitudes. An Aboriginal field officer with CAALAS in 1975, Peter Rotumah, recorded his impression of this:

> The first one was the segregating, the categorising of Aboriginal people. The categorising of Aboriginal and European people in the hospital, and the segregating of Aboriginal people from Europeans in the hospital wards. The second was the general attitude – I suppose, of non-Aboriginal people to the people in the fringe-camps and the tribal people was 'Jack's all right as long as he stays in his place. If he moves out, then it's not his place to move out'.[4]

By 1975 community tensions had escalated to breaking point, leading to the outbreak of violence between whites and blacks, proposals for vigilante groups and intense lobbying of the federal government by local white residents. A CAALAS lawyer recalled the level of fear at the time:

> We thought very seriously about arming ourselves, simply because there were vigilante squads being interviewed on the talkback radio up there about how they were arming themselves for the black invasion of Alice Springs … Yes, it was a very aggressive, very nasty time when whites were being for the first time challenged by Aboriginal people who had spokespeople who were prepared to go to court and say 'No, this isn't right,' and 'No, it can be done in a different way'.[5]

Given the situation in Alice Springs from the mid-1960s it was a tragic inevitability that authorities should look to the practice of forcibly removing Aboriginal children from their families as a solution to the continuing stalemate in Alice Springs camps. Aboriginal children in the Northern Territory were already predisposed to be by far the main population affected by legislation such as the *Child Welfare Ordinance 1958* that was intended notionally to be applied to the general population of the Territory – that is, it was not an Aboriginal-specific ordinance. Because their families constituted the majority of disadvantaged and destitute people, Aboriginal children were more likely to fit the criteria of 'neglected child' to official eyes than non-Aboriginal children as a whole. Indeed the Ordinance was used, in the mid-1960s at least, for purposes other than its objective of protecting the best interests of Aboriginal children.

As well as fitting in with enduring assimilationist perspectives that separating Aboriginal children from their cultural communities was desirable, removal was infinitely cheaper and easier for governments than embarking on the major social reconstruction programs that could have helped communities and families to recover stability and security. The record of the threats to Aboriginal parents and children in Alice Springs also reads as a series of government and townsfolk campaigns to keep Aboriginal people out of town.

This is evident in the fact that following the removal of formal powers in 1964 to control Aboriginal movements, the Northern Territory government resorted to using the *Child Welfare Ordinance 1958* to limit the presence of Aboriginal people in Alice Springs. In 1965 the Director of Welfare,

Harry Giese, in a letter to the Director of Health, signalled his intention to use the ordinance to attempt to break up town camps:

I propose so far as families with children are concerned, and where the children are obviously not regularly attending school to have the Children's Court commit the children to my care as neglected children, but this will not completely solve the problem because there are a number of families without children living in this area.[6]

In a particularly revealing document, Welfare Branch officer, T. C. Lovegrove (signing for his superior, L. N. Penhall), reported to his Director on the operation of this tactic in 1966:

Some children have been taken before the court and some [families] have been persuaded to leave Alice Springs upon being threatened that the provisions of the Child Welfare Ordinance will be used.[7]

After detailing cases where twenty-seven children were removed from the town with the deliberate intention of making their town-camping parents leave as well, Lovegrove continued:

Pressures will continue to be applied in accordance with your instructions. This will only go part of the way towards solving the problems of unsightly camps in the Alice Springs area and if there is a genuine desire to solve this problem persons outside of the Welfare Branch will have to co-operate by doing some hard thinking and hard acting on the problem.[8]

Despite this open admission, three years later in 1969 Lovegrove, now Assistant Director, wrote to District Welfare Officers, in effect to caution them on the too overt use of the Ordinance as a means of removing town campers:

> I think some members of the public are conscious of this and generally concerned. For the person viewing the situation from a distance this appears to be and often is the case and there have been a number of children prosecuted as 'Neglected' in these circumstances.[9]

But despite what Lovegrove claimed was genuine concern for the welfare of children by 'members of the public', he went on to reinforce the fact that the primary concern was to remove campers, for which the Ordinance was, in any case, not always effective:

> This has the effect of removing the child from the situation but does not necessarily remove the rest of the family and it has no effect when there are no children involved. Furthermore, it must not be used automatically on families living in these conditions. The case must be one of severe and immediately irretrievable neglect. I suggest that it was never intended that this piece of legislation be used to solve the municipal problems of any township.[10]

Lovegrove revealed himself to be part of that same 'concerned' Alice Spring's 'public'. Town campers should be shifted because:

> [their] mode of living is substandard and aesthetically offensive to a majority of townspeople. This may be a valid complaint but I doubt if it is a violation of any law applicable to the town. If we are honest we will admit that this is our main complaint. (In using 'our' I am identifying myself as one of the townspeople of Alice Springs.)[11]

Lovegrove went on to advocate the introduction of appropriate and transparent legislation that would allow his department to deal effectively with the 'municipal problems' of offensive behaviour and concern about health threats instead of having to resort to child welfare legislation:

> There should be legislation to deal with it. If there is legislation then it should be put into effect. If it is inadequate or non-existent then the [Health] Department should be proposing legislation that will deal with the problem.[12]

The broad definition of 'neglect' in the *Child Welfare Ordinance 1958* was open to culturally biased or ethnocentric interpretation and application on the part of individual officers, the judiciary, police and medical professionals. Also, because there were no formal mechanisms for Aboriginal advice on what constituted neglect, child care circumstances that were culturally acceptable to Aboriginal people could be determined as unacceptable by non-Aboriginal officials working from the perspective of their ideals. Moreover, failure to recognise Aboriginal family arrangements and patterns of child-care ensured that the alternative of placing children in the care of their extended families was rarely considered. That there were cases where the extended family was unable to provide the alternative care because whole families had become destitute points us to the larger political and economic contexts. The removal of children from their families was an administrative measure that reflected the failure of government to tackle what was obviously a social disaster of great proportions. Bureaucratic thinking and policy proceeded with the expectation that Aboriginal people were to adopt the standards of an ideal non-Aboriginal norm inherent to the assimilation vision. Not only was this profoundly ethnocentric, but it was a practical impossibility for the majority in Alice Springs after decades of impoverishment and exclusion from the resources and institutions of Australian society.

In 1973, when Warren Braedon was born, the situation appears to have been desperate for many Aboriginal people living in the camps in the town. Town campers like Dawna Braedon and her family were under constant pressure to move out of the town area through a combination of heavy policing of drinking, public panics over health, and the removal of children by welfare authorities. The failure of local authorities and the Northern Territory administration to improve the campers' health and welfare problems appears to have owed more to the desire to simply remove the people from the town, than to any insurmountable practical factors.

The rationale of the policy of assimilation was that Aboriginal people were to live like other Australians – in houses, as nuclear families, in regular employment and schooling. The method of forcing this change was institutionalisation – the relocation of families to missions and government settlements and the removal of children. But as the CAAC statement above indicates, Aboriginal people were not opposed to living in houses per se. They were not, as a rule, opposed to using the sanitation systems suited to more sedentary populations. They did, however, resist the breaking-up of their extended families and restrictions on their freedom of movement and traditional cultural practices. Ways needed to be found to make the social technologies of sanitation, housing and health care adaptable to contemporary Indigenous lifestyles and traditions. This was the thrust of CAAC's and Tangentyere's strategies. From the mid-1970s the implementation of these strategies started to take effect – too late, however, to make a difference to Dawna Braedon's capacity to keep her family together.

The Braedon family

Warren Braedon was born in Alice Springs on 4 January 1973 to Dawna Braedon and Joe Johnson, Dawna a Luritja woman (of the Napajinpa skin group) and Joe an Arrernte man. Warren's Dreaming was the eagle from Titjikala (Maryvale Station).[1] The Arrernte peoples are the traditional owners of the Alice Springs region. The land on which the town stands is known as Mparntwe. The Arrernte language group comprises five or six major interrelated groups distinguished from each other by geographic territory and variations in dialect, customs and religious beliefs. The Luritja occupy country that mainly borders on that of the Western and Southern Arrernte, to the west and south of Alice Springs. A distinct language group from the Arrernte, the Luritja often intermarry with them and share some facets of ceremony and custom. Traditional Arrernte and Luritja societies are based on communal hunting and gathering. The main social and economic unit is the extended family, with each family living independently of each other on their separate estates. Families travel within their estates for ceremonial and economic purposes, and congregate with others for larger ceremonies. Hagen states that 'for the Aranda [Arrernte], law, convention and morality are intimately linked to the land through the actions of their ancestors'.[2] These were autonomous, self-governing societies, with complex social and legal and spiritual systems. Just as firm laws and social and cultural precepts governed the relations between groups and individuals within each group, so they also governed the manner in which individuals and groups used the resources of the fragile environment.[3]

Dawna's father was an Arrernte man, Toby Braedon, from Titjikala.[4] Her mother was a Matuntara woman, Tilly, from Tempe Downs.[5] The couple had six children: Dorothy, Dawna, Valerie, Raylene, Ernest and Eric.[6] These children produced at least twenty-four grandchildren between them – Warren's siblings and cousins. At his home in Little Sisters Camp in 1996 Eric, Dawna's brother, recalls:

> My father used to work here and my sisters grew up here. He worked night and day, went out in this old truck, didn't work for money, just got tucker, to bring all my sisters up. He was one of the wise old men, he even knew everyone's Dreaming. They come and ask him. He knew everything.[7]

Eric's niece, Mary Williams, daughter of Dawna's sister Valerie, describes Toby's important role as an elder:

> Everyone that forgot about their Dreaming, they'd come and he'd tell them, he told them all. Even Hermannsburg, you

know how the missionaries made them not want to do that thing any more, they forgot that Dreaming, he could tell them their Dreaming. He'd just ask, 'Tell me what family group you're from,' and he'd just tell them, sing that story and all. He was really a wise old man, he knew everything. Any family group they just come and talk … and he'd know, 'Oh you're from this country,' tell them.[8]

Eric states that Toby's cousin Max Stuart and son-in-law Casey Kenny are now the custodians of these Dreaming stories.[9]

Prior to the establishment of a sewerage system in Alice Springs during the 1950s, local contractors employed Aboriginal people in sanitary and rubbish collection from the town. Some of those employed lived at Little Sisters Camp, including the Braedons. Little Sisters was used during the 1940s by sanitary workers servicing the town's wartime-inflated population.[10] Dawna's son, Kevin, describes Toby's work as a sewerage truck driver:

Old grandfather, Toby, from here, when he was young he used to work here in town getting that, bucket of thing, shit carting, bring around the toilets getting that bucket in the laneway, driving. He had a license for driving, working for something for one pound a day. That's when we was talking he was telling me that, this story, working and this old, what they used, bucket and they had this big trench to empty it at – take it back, come round, put it back in the same place, drive around. He did that for a long time when he was young.

His kids grew up with him. They went to school. Mum went to Telegraph Station, Bungalow to school and come home again, didn't have to live there. She went to school and then she met up with Dad. Here. That's when they had me. He was from station, working out at Nappa Station, a stockman. That was his country.[11]

A former resident at Little Sisters described their lives:

We lived in humpies all in a line. The families there were all one big family, the fathers all worked hard and were working till they died. They didn't know what the dole was. The kids all went to Old Harley Street Primary (but not Dawna). We went to grade seven in those days. All the kids knew each other, went to same school. We all called our uncles 'father' and they all helped look after the kids. We got meat, tripe from the old slaughter yards. We were poor and ragged but we shared everything. Our mothers didn't turn kids away, we shared everything.[12]

Toby lived to a very old age and died of pneumonia at the Hettie Perkins Hostel in 1992.

Eric Braedon was raised by his sisters, principally Dawna, who nursed him along with her own baby, Kevin:

When I was a newborn baby we was sharing walytja [breast], we was both sharing, he was on this side and I was on this side. That happens a lot, it's Aboriginal way. So it was my sister that brought me up. So Dawna was sort of my mother too. As I got older she handed me to my mother's cousin and she brought me up, Phyllis Whistle. I call her mother. She brought me up from when I was a little boy.[13]

Dawna had grown up in Alice Springs camps with her parents. She gave birth to five children: Kevin, who lives in Alice Springs, Vincent, Ricky, Jaclyn and Warren.[14] All except Kevin were taken away from her. She was sixteen when Kevin was born in Alice Springs Hospital in 1961, during a period when she was working as a housekeeper at Tempe Downs Station. Kevin recalls these early years:

I grew up with my Mother and Dad. They got separated, I was raised up by my grandfather [Toby Braedon], the one in the cemetery there, and from there I was raised up by my mother's young sister Valerie. From there she started looking after me. I was a little fella when I went to her and then I went to school out at Amoonguna. We were stopping out at there, went to school there first. Mum and Dad went separate ways. From there Mum went out to Western Australia, she come back with Jaclyn and from there she had Ricky and they were taken away. Then she went back to Western Australia again. From there she came back to Alice Springs that's where she had Louis.

She married out there [Western Australia], another man, from Derby and I heard he passed away. Used to go there by plane, flying over. When Mum came back when she had Louis she went back to the Aboriginal reserve [Amoonguna] seven miles out from here where I was. She started drinking again from there.[15]

Eric Braedon says that Dawna began drinking heavily when her children were taken from her. Ricky and Jaclyn were both removed from her custody and are presumed to have been adopted or fostered.[16] Another older son, Vincent, was apparently placed with an Aboriginal family in the late 1960s in Santa Teresa Mission. Only Kevin grew up within his extended family in Alice Springs, on pastoral stations, and at Amoonguna government settlement. He kept in contact with his mother but lived primarily with his aunt Valerie. In addition to English, Kevin speaks Luritja, Arrernte and Pitjantjatjara.

I went off working on the stations. I went with my uncle to Amburla Station [west of Alice Springs], a bit close, one day trip and back again. Working out there then. We had this cattle coming in from Queensland, all the little calves, for transport. Had to shift them bore to bore, riding horses. I was fourteen. Because I didn't want to really go to school, just wanted to go out bush. We had a cook and a Land Rover and trailer with everything on, spare saddles, bridles and some tin stuff, go bore to bore shifting all the calves. I was with family, working out there. I was learning hunting and how to, teaching me how to brand calves. I did that for six months straight just come in for weekend to Alice Springs and back out, do a bit of shopping, see family.[17]

This was 1975. After six months Kevin returned to Alice Springs and then went back to Amoonguna. Life at the government settlement was desolate for the young men. Frustrated, Kevin soon came into conflict with authorities.

I was working out on the reserve for a long time. I was rubbish collecting, driving around in the tractor. I just went mad, rolled that drum of diesel, rolled it down to the wall, starting tipping it over, let all the diesel spill out and push it back again and strike a match and the just ... That's when they found out that I did it and went to court for it and they tried to sentence me to twelve months to some children's prison, Essington House, in Darwin. And so one of these old ladies, she's one of the welfare, came. She used to work out at Amoonguna, fighting, so she had to fight for me so they had to drop the sentence to six months, to spend six months at Darwin. They had to send me by plane, my first time. I was scared.[18]

When Kevin returned to Alice Springs, he lived in a camp and worked as a rubbish collector at Amoonguna. As people moved away from the settlement, Kevin went to stay with his grandfather and other relatives at Maryvale Station. During this time Kevin was taught about his grandfather's country.

I was stopping there for my grandfather, there's two grand-fathers, one buried here and one buried out at Maryvale. I was stopping with him just like looking after him, working out there sitting down, just going out hunting and all, camping out and grandfather was showing me all these Dreaming sites you know, things. This rainbow snake they was marking it all the way. That's my grandfather's country out there. He was showing me where they going to make this outstation [Titjikala].[19]

In 1986 Dawna was admitted to hospital with a chronic neurological disorder, and lost the power of speech. At the time Kevin was staying with her and other family members at Little Sisters Camp. The following year she was placed in Hettie Perkins Hostel. Kevin described Dawna's treatment by ambulance attendants:

> That's when she had that stroke and she couldn't even move at all. She was lying there and this ambulance man come round there and they thought she was drunk because her eye was red. And like, my grandfather and uncle they was talking to the ambulance driver, 'She's not drunk at all, she just had a stroke. Can't you see?' She was just lying down there so they had to put her in and, you know, to hospital. I don't know how long she spent in hospital there.[20]

Two years later, Kevin's younger brother Vincent was accidentally driven over and killed while he was camped just outside Santa Teresa Mission. He left a wife and two boys.

> They were drinking too much and another bloke on the Toyota he didn't know that my young brother was in front asleep. So he took off and just runned over him. So he had to pass away too. He was lying on the ground in front of the Toyota.[21]

Tragically, details of these two incidents would be repeated in the events surrounding Warren Braedon's death in Perth in 1992.

Removal

Warren Braedon was committed to state custody in early 1973 under the Northern Territory's *Child Welfare Ordinance 1958*, following an application by the Department of Child Welfare to the Southern District Children's Court. The Northern Territory government had, to the original time of writing in 1999, refused to release documents that would clarify the precise steps that were taken in Warren's case. For instance, the official grounds for his removal remained locked in his file. Legal correspondence held by the Johnson family indicates that Dawna had been arrested for drunkenness on numerous occasions from 1971 to 1973, and that two departmental reports provided 'very substantial grounds for the Officer's belief that the mother has neglected her child Warren'.[1] A Court Order was issued in Alice Springs to the effect that Warren was 'a neglected child' and he was committed to the care of the Director of Child Welfare.[2] As a 'State child' Warren would remain under the Director's guardianship until the age of eighteen.³ Presumably, Warren had then been placed in the Welfare Receiving Home in Alice Springs. He was then sent to Dundas House, a receiving institution in Darwin. It is not known whether the Department made any effort to find care or placement for Warren in his extended family or in any other Aboriginal family. Kevin explains that Dawna's drinking, which began after the removal of Ricky and Jaclyn, was to play an important role in the removal of her youngest child Warren – removal which went ahead despite her objections and her persistent refusal to give her permission for his adoption.

> She had her sister there, the one who look after me but was too sick to look after Louis, so she started reporting to the welfare because she had kids of her own and that's when welfare went round and had a talk with Mum there and they said, 'Oh we have to take Louis away because you're drinking too much, you can't look after him'. She didn't say nothing, couldn't do anything, because there were some police there you know too. And from there they took Louis away. He was still a little baby. Then we didn't see him again.⁴

Mary Williams, who helped to raise Kevin, says:

> Just that she had a drinking problem, that's all. But she was a good mother. Now it's all right, I was working with [a government organisation] ... for four months and the last thing they do is take them off their mother, especially Aboriginal family they have to find a way of talking to the mother first, try and straighten things out. They don't want to do what they

did before. They're trying to change that now. They wouldn't have talked to anyone, just taken him away, same with the other two children.[5]

Adoption

Warren Braedon was put up for adoption under the Northern Territory's *Adoption of Children Ordinance 1964*. This ordinance, like the Social Welfare and Child Welfare ordinances, did not have a special formal application to Aboriginal children but applied to children generally. Legal adoption of Aboriginal children was rare in the Northern Territory until the late 1950s. Prior to this children were placed in institutions or apprenticed to employers. During the 1950s and 1960s adoption and, to a lesser extent, fostering, were seen by many as the best means of assimilation into white society for babies and young children (older children were generally not favoured by adoptive parents). In this way, the Ordinance's 'paramount consideration' of ' the best interests of the child' was axiomatic with an upbringing in a white home. As with the Child Welfare ordinances – and partly because of them, since state wards were often fed into the adoption process – Aboriginal children were far more likely to come under the adoption jurisdiction. Louis was a case of involuntary adoption in the strict sense. It is clear that Dawna did not give her consent to his adoption since the Director of Child Welfare was obliged to take action in the Northern Territory Supreme Court to have her consent dispensed with.[1]

The government resorted to promotional campaigns in the press and within churches, to attract prospective adoptive parents.[2] Non-Aboriginal couples were the targets of this program. Various factors precluded Aboriginal people from adopting any children, let alone those from their own community. Given the assimilationist intent of the adoption program, it was unlikely that children would be placed with Aboriginal applicants,[3] and the Ordinance's broad selection criteria for adoptive parents provided a ready way to exclude them.[4] Adoption in the western legal sense of transferring permanent custody conflicted with Aboriginal family systems and values and this may have deterred Aboriginal couples from applying. Without even considering the rationales of the departmental and judicial decision makers, the actual operation of both the Adoption and Social Welfare ordinances illustrates how government instruments, that are notionally egalitarian and universalist, can be structurally inequitable. Inequality of outcomes is virtually guaranteed because such policies and legislation cannot recognise either the existing cultural difference or the economic disparity that predispose certain populations to be disproportionately affected by them.

It was only from the late 1970s, through Aboriginal and welfare agency pressure, that major changes in policy and practice – to attend to cultural and economic differences

– began. The Aboriginal child placement principle, which guided these changes, stated that Aboriginal children should remain with their family and community environments, and that removal of any Aboriginal children should be a last resort. It called for the recognition of Indigenous customs relating to child care, the review of existing welfare practices and services, and the development of Aboriginal family support programs – all for the purpose of keeping the children within their birth families. Where removal was seen to be the only course of action, fostering and adoption should be within Aboriginal families only. Aboriginal advice to governments on adoption issues was to be formalised and Aboriginal services for families and child placement agencies were set up in all states.[5]

These national developments were reflected in the Northern Territory government's child welfare reviews and reforms from 1978. They coincided with the Territory's change to self-government in 1978, and a determination to revamp the welfare system, which had been the butt of public criticism from the early 1970s. The Department of Community Development was created with a Community Welfare Division mandated to provide child and family services. In 1979 the report of the Martin Inquiry into welfare recommended the repeal of the Social Welfare Ordinance and the introduction of new legislation to promote individual, family and community welfare.[6] The Northern Territory *Community Welfare Act 1983* enshrined the Aboriginal Child Placement Principle: that is, 'the best interests' of Aboriginal children were met by allowing them to remain in their own families and communities – the first Australian legislation to do so.[7]

The shift in attitudes toward Aboriginal child adoptions is illustrated by a judgment on child custody handed down by the Northern Territory Supreme Court in 1976 that actually went in favour of the Aboriginal mother.[8] This was only two years after the Court had agreed to the legal adoption of Warren Braedon. The case involved the application to the Court by an American couple based in Alice Springs to dispense with the consent of the Aboriginal birth mother whose child they wished to adopt. The mother was represented by the Central Australian Aboriginal Legal Aid Service (CAALAS). The two-year-old baby boy had been committed to the care of the Director of Child Welfare as a neglected child in May 1975. In the same month the baby was given to the American couple to foster. However, in this case the court did not grant the application. Justice Forster noted that Section 10 of the Adoption of Children Ordinance directed that the 'welfare and interests of the child be regarded as paramount'.

The Judge considered that the only grounds on which he could dispense with consent would be if the advantages to the child of being adopted by the white foster parents amounted to special circumstances. While the foster parents could offer the child love and security within their family, the mother could offer him 'the love of his natural mother and an extended family in which, as he grows older, he will probably feel more at home than with a white family'. It was further found that the living conditions that the child would enjoy with his mother 'would, by European standards, be considerably less than those offered by the foster parents. However, by Aboriginal standards they are perfectly adequate'. The judge concluded that what was offered by the foster parents in a material, emotional, spiritual way was not superior to what the mother could offer and ordered that the child be returned to the mother's care.[9]

Forster was also critical of the way that staff of the Northern Territory Department of Social Welfare had handled the committal application to the Children's Court. They had failed to properly notify and explain their intentions to the boy's mother and as a result she was not able to attend the hearing and hence to represent her interests. He found that this constituted 'a denial of justice of a particularly serious kind'.[10] He also criticised their failure to provide the court with a report on the mother's present circumstances, that is, information that would support or refute the claim that she was incapable of caring for her son. As a result, the Department could not 'confirm or deny' the evidence presented by the mother's witnesses that the boy should be returned to her care. The Children's Court ruling was that the mother had neglected the baby, however, the judge was unable to find that she had persistently done so in the past or would do so in the future. On the other hand, it was evident that the mother had gone to great lengths to find her son and the judge was satisfied that she loved and wanted him.

The case was also significant for Justice Forster's recognition of the serious problems associated with cross-cultural adoptions. He expressed concern that if the boy grew up with a white family in America he would:

> undergo an identity crisis when he realised that he is different in appearance to the people who surround him. Quite apart from any racial problems which he may encounter in the

United States he is likely to encounter problems arising within himself because of the very fact that his physical appearance is different.[11]

Forster accepted expert evidence that the child's best interest was served by having him remain with his mother and within his community. He found that although material conditions may have been less substantial than the foster parents could provide, they were nonetheless adequate and were more than outweighed by the advantages of a loving and caring extended family, and of being a fully accepted member of an Aboriginal community. The CAALAS lawyer, Ross Howie, reflected on the significance of the decision:

It challenged the assumptions of the way the system worked, because instead of Aboriginals being lined up in court and asked whether they pleaded guilty, and everybody nodding and being dealt with, people started having the rights that other Australian citizens have, and that is to have advice and to make decisions and to fight cases and to be found not guilty. Similarly, not only the criminal justice system but the welfare system, which like all systems, I suppose, tended to make patronising decisions about people who didn't have much power, regardless of what their rights were or whether they ought to be heard about the matter. And one of the good things about the court's decision was that His Honour was critical of the magistrate and critical of the Welfare Department, and criticisms like that change how things happen.[12]

The Johnsons

Bill and Pauline Johnson arrived in Australia from England in 1972. They were living at Nhunlunbuy on the Gove Peninsula, Northern Territory, when they applied to adopt a child. They were told that it was easy to adopt an Aboriginal child, but the government officer handling their enquiries, a Mr Taylor, advised them against it because 'they just cause trouble'. They responded that:

> one child is very much like another and we were happy to adopt an Aboriginal child as much as a white child. We didn't understand at that time what we were getting involved in. We didn't understand the damage that was done by cross-cultural adoption and the part that cross-cultural adoption played in the enforced assimilation policy that was still being practiced at that time. So we did, as far as we were concerned, we did involve ourselves in a grave injustice to Aboriginal people and a grave injustice to Louis and his family, and obviously

we recognise now, we have since apologised for the wrong that we caused and the injustice that we were involved in. Obviously that doesn't help Louis' family at all.[1]

The officer informed the Johnsons that they would be placed on the official adoption list and that a baby who would not be 'too dark' would soon be available.[2]

The Johnsons first saw Warren at the receiving home, Dundas House, in Darwin in 1973. He was three months old and weighed twelve pounds. He was described to them as 'a hard to place child' and they were told that he had hearing problems and a heart condition, although subsequent medical tests showed that he was in perfect health. They were also informed that he had been declared a 'neglected child' by the Alice Springs Court and committed to the care of the Director of Child Welfare. A month later the baby was handed to the couple on the understanding that they could adopt him. Bill recalled that:

When we were introduced to him he had above his cot the [name] 'baby Warren'. We said to the two nurses and the social worker who introduced us, he was just lying in the cot, 'Is that his real name because we will keep it'. They said, 'No, no, don't worry about that, that's just the name that the nurses have given him'.

I think that was one of the nastiest things about Louis' adoption – that Warren Braedon was actually his name. We found out when we took him back to Alice Springs for burial, and you know it wasn't sufficient for them to strip him of his family and all connections with his family but they even had to strip his name from him.[3]

Both twenty-eight years of age, Bill and Pauline were taken through the adoption process by the Department of Child Welfare. Dawna had not given her consent to the adoption and the Director of Child Welfare applied to the Supreme Court to have it dispensed with. The Department had told the Johnsons that the baby had been abandoned three times by his mother and that this was sufficient reason for him to be removed. Encouraging the couple to push ahead with the adoption, officials spoke of Warren's family, and Aboriginal people in general, in 'dismissive, almost derogatory terms'.[4] Bill and Pauline had him in their care for sixteen months before the order was made by the Supreme Court to dispense with Dawna's consent. In an emotional verbal submission to the Inquiry into the Separation of the Aboriginal and Torres Strait Islander Children from their Families in 1996, Bill stated:

> so you can see that we participated in something that was doubly unjust, you know. To take a child away, to participate in an adoption that may be seen to be to the child's benefit, is one thing, but to actually participate in an adoption that was specifically against the mother's wishes is doubly unjust. Anyway in our ignorance – and that's the only justification, the only excuse we've got – that's what happened. Our reaction was, well his mother doesn't want him, we'll give him a good home and he is going to be advantaged rather than disadvantaged by the separation.

Why the hell couldn't they have placed him with an Aboriginal family or into an Aboriginal background? I don't know, because it did happen with [his brother] Vincent.[5]

Reflecting on their thinking at the time, Bill believes that had they looked more deeply into Warren's background and the adoption issue, they may have acted differently.

We were just blinded by the fact that we wanted a child. I don't believe that we considered Louis' mother's position objectively or even subjectively by putting ourselves in her position, and if we had taken the time to do so then we may have done that, and we should have come up with a different decision.[6]

Irrespective of the couple's desire to have Warren, they believed, and they had been convinced by the Department, that they were doing the right thing by him. Indeed, they were led to believe that they were saving his life, such was the departmental representation of his unseen mother. Giving the couple the child without Dawna's consent to an adoption should never have occurred in a legal state adoption. Furthermore, the Department should have been entirely responsible for handling any legal issues arising.[7]

In October 1973 the Johnsons moved to Sydney with the baby and in the following year they moved to Perth. The couple received a telegram on 27 August 1974 from their solicitor informing them that their application for the adoption order in the Northern Territory Supreme Court had been successful. The judge's grounds for dispensing with Dawna's consent were that he 'was satisfied that ... the mother had abandoned the child and had neglected the child'.[8] Under the conditions of the Adoption Ordinance Warren was renamed Louis St John Johnson and his birth certificate was altered to show the Johnsons as his birth parents. With Bill following work in the construction industry, the family moved back to the Northern Territory for a period, then to Sydney again, before returning to Perth to settle permanently in 1978.

Louis at five and a half months, Gove NT 1973.

Louis at approximately seven and a half months, with his adoptive parents Bill and Pauline Johnson, Gove NT 1973.

Louis in the bath at approximately five months, Gove NT.

Louis as a toddler.

Louis and Pauline in England 1975.

Louis and Bill in North Wales 1975.

Louis with his adoptive sister, Bethan, and Pauline camping at Lancelin WA 1977.

Louis, going on six, and Bethan, four years old.

Louis with cousins Jake and Toby and uncle Jim, Sydney NSW.

Louis sitting on his surfboard, Manly NSW.

Louis at Christmas.

Louis with his adoptive siblings, Bethan and Tony, Jamaica 1983.

Louis, going on eight, Perth WA.

Louis in his school uniform, Perth WA.

Louis with his siblings at Christmas, England 1984.

Louis at fourteen with brand new akubra, Alice Springs.

Louis returned to Alice Springs in 1987 in an attempt to find his birth family.

Louis with his family, Perth WA.

Louis at sixteen and a half, with Pauline in North Wales, after completing an outdoor adventure course (Outward Bound).

Louis with nanna Blake.

Louis at Scarborough Beach, Perth WA.

Louis riding in Gnangara forest WA, just turned eighteen.

Louis with cousins Jake and Toby.

WARREN BRAEDEN

SON OF DAWNA BRAEDEN

NAMED BY HIS ADOPTIVE PARENTS
LOUIS ST. JOHN JOHNSON

*HE NEVER KNEW HIS NAME
HE NEVER KNEW HIS MOTHER
HE NEVER KNEW HIS FAMILY
HE NEVER KNEW HIS PEOPLE
HE NEVER KNEW HIS COUNTRY*

BORN ALICE SPRINGS
4TH JANUARY, 1973
MURDERED PERTH, W.A.
4TH JANUARY, 1992
. . . . .BECAUSE HE WAS BLACK

RETURNED TO HIS FAMILY AND HIS COUNTRY
20TH JANUARY, 1992

HE HAS FOUND HIS DREAMING

*"WRAP ME IN THE MOTHER EARTH
SO I CAN NURTURE THE LAND'S REBIRTH
GIVE ME JOY AND GIVE ME SONG
CARRY THE STRUGGLE WIDE AND LONG"*
(KEV CARMODY)

"BEAUTIFUL, BEAUTIFUL CHILD NOW YOU ARE FREE
FREE FROM THIS HEARTACHE AND PAIN AND MISERY. . . .
. . . . I WISH I WAS WITH YOU RIGHT NOW,
MY BEAUTIFUL CHILD"
(ARCHIE ROACH)

Louis' epitaph at Alice Springs Cemetery.

Louis' funeral was attended by his extended Braedon family. Louis' birth mother Dawna and his grandfather are pictured sitting either side of Pauline. Dawna was buried with Louis when she died some years later—united in death.

Archie Roach performing in Forrest Place, Perth WA.

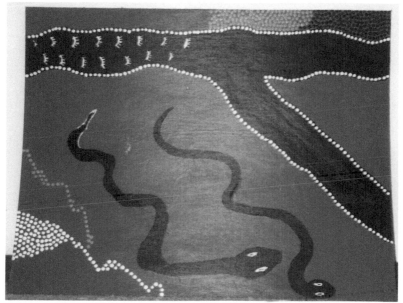

One of the paintings that Louis was working on, but never finished, before his death.

Perth

The city to which the Johnsons brought young Louis in 1978 seemed to hold the promise of a better life for all. It was the fastest growing capital in the country, with a beautiful river and coastal setting and a strong economic base in the state's mineral resource wealth. Although Perth did not like to think of itself as a particularly discriminatory place, as having a 'race' problem in the sense of American or British cities, the reality for many Aboriginal people said otherwise. The statistics on incarceration alone demonstrated the gulf between the ideal of general prosperity and this reality. In 1981, the Aboriginal imprisonment rate in Western Australia was 1448 per 100,000 compared with 109 per 100,000 for non-Aboriginal people, the highest rate of Aboriginal incarceration, by far, of any state.[1] Moreover, by 1987 Aboriginal teenagers made up about sixty per cent of the inmates of juvenile detention centres, while they comprised only four per cent of the state's child population.[2] Of the ninety-nine cases of Aboriginal deaths

in custody between 1980 and 1989 investigated by the Royal
Commission into Aboriginal Deaths in Custody (RCIADIC),
thirty-two occurred in Western Australia. The Equal
Opportunity Commission (1989) and RCIADIC (1991) found
that police harassment of Aboriginal people, and particularly
Aboriginal youth, was a serious problem in Western Australia.[3]

In almost every other area of life too, Aboriginal people
suffered massive inequalities. In 1981 Western Australia had
the second highest official rate of Aboriginal unemployment
of any state at 30.9 per cent, compared to the state's overall
unemployment rate of 6.3 per cent.[4] Their infant mortality
rate in 1980 was 31.3 per cent.[5] In 1984 over 54 per cent of
children in foster care placements in Western Australia were
Aboriginal, while 58 per cent of children in residential child
care establishments were Aboriginal.[6] Educational levels were
also disastrous. In 1983 only forty-eight Aboriginal children
in Western Australia made it into Year 12 high school, a
retention rate of 4.5 per cent.[7] By 1987 this had improved to
10.2 per cent but was still far below the 57.1 per cent for the
total population.[8] In the south west of the state only thirteen
students reached Year 12 in 1988.[9] Indigenous dispossession
in Western Australia was almost total. For example, in 1981,
apart from land purchased as private citizens, the original
inhabitants held freehold title to only thirty square kilometres
out of a total land mass of two-and-a-half million square
kilometres.[10] Lands were available as reserves and leases for
Aboriginal use, but not ownership, and the vast majority
of these were located in the northern and western regions
of the state even though one third of the state's Indigenous
population lived in the capital and southern region.

Public attitudes towards Aboriginal people in Western Australia in the early 1980s were the most hostile of any state. The 1984 Australian National Opinion Poll survey of attitudes found that:

> Fears and prejudices are much the same across Australia, but they are more pronounced in the West and the North.[11]

More Western Australians were strongly opposed to land rights (43 per cent compared to only 6 per cent strongly in favour) than in other states.[12] More believed that Aboriginal people received too much government assistance (69 per cent),[13] and many were unable to nominate a single Aboriginal person they were 'particularly impressed with' (49 per cent).[14] Anti-land rights publicity campaigns by the mining industry and the Liberal Party in the mid-1980s did much to spread and harden such attitudes. This was only made worse by openly discriminatory actions by successive governments, notably the trampling on Aboriginal religion and sacred areas in Noonkanbah in 1980, the Harding Dam in 1984 and, from 1989, the Old Swan Brewery in Perth.

Since the 1950s, many Noongar families had moved into the metropolitan area from country towns seeking a better life, mainly in terms of employment, housing and schooling.[15] This urban movement occurred because of a combination of assimilation policies and prejudice and exclusion in rural areas and a fall in employment due to the drop in rural labour demands. However, by the late 1970s, with the decrease in manufacturing industries, prospects of stable employment and job training declined for Noongar families in Perth. Growing unemployment was particularly severe amongst youth. Sixty-three per cent of Aboriginal people in Western Australia were under the age of twenty-four in 1986.[16] Economic deprivation and all the social problems associated with it, such as delinquency and substance abuse, were exacerbated by widespread prejudice and indifference in Perth society. This included denial of Aboriginal cultural identity. The 1984 Western Australian Aboriginal Land Inquiry Commissioner put his finger on a particular white perception of Noongar people:

> There is a sense in which Europeans do not see Nyungars [sic] as being real Aborigines because they do not have the overt trappings of what Europeans have decided is a typical Aboriginal lifestyle. The Nyungars take a different view. Although they live in a European environment they retain a strong consciousness of their own identities as Nyungars. They draw a firm contrast between Nyungar and Wetjala (white fella) ways especially between Nyungar and Wetjala values.[17]

Both Coalition and Labor governments had failed to develop and implement appropriate programs to address the problems of Noongar youth.[18] By the end of the 1980s they had become demonised in the Perth public domain by the police, media and politicians. The Director of the Western Australian Aboriginal Legal Service Rob Riley stated in 1990:

> You can imagine the effect this sort of reporting is having on young Aboriginal people around the city, going to school or work, or just walking down the street. It would be very

difficult to feel positive about yourself or that other people were going to have a positive attitude toward you.[19]

Louis Johnson was not a Noongar, nor was he poor. But he was young and Aboriginal. He had to go to school, to work, and of course 'just walk down the street' in the capital city of the state with the worst regard for its Indigenous citizens.

Life in Perth

The Johnsons recall Louis having a happy early childhood. He was contented and 'didn't have a care in the world'.[20] In 1978 Louis started at St John's Catholic Primary School in Scarborough and later transferred to the Holy Rosary Primary School at Wembley. Even though these were happy years for the boy, the effects of racial prejudice were to increasingly affect Louis and indeed the whole family. Pauline had already been the butt of racist taunts from members of the public in Darwin and Perth who presumably thought that Louis was her son to an Aboriginal man. As she wheeled baby Louis along in his pram she was spat upon by men and verbally abused by women muttering that this 'shouldn't be allowed to happen' and by people in cars calling out 'boong' and 'nigger'.[21] As Bill reflects:

> We could see the prejudice that he was always meeting in those early years because you go out with an Aboriginal child, boy, youth and stand back, you can see the prejudice that they are meeting every day of their lives. It's either overt or it's covert, it's a raised eyebrow, it can be anything, people looking down their noses at kids. They can express it in many different ways.[22]

When Louis started at Newman College in Doubleview in 1986, at the age of thirteen, he came to experience more unrelenting racism because of his Aboriginality. The relative happiness of his primary school years turned into increasing misery and hurt. This is evidenced in a homework assignment in which he was asked to list his likes and dislikes. 'I like most of the teachers, I like Brother Joe, I like the people in the school office, I like science, maths, TD, English. I like the Year 9 girls, boy! I like the music class'.[23] For his dislikes, Louis wrote down the names of four boys who called him 'boong, petrol-sniffer, Abo and nigger'. Pauline recalls that from this time she became increasingly protective of Louis and exercised 'one hundred per cent vigilance' to protect him from harassment. It became evident that the other students would often set Louis up to get him into trouble and that he would be blamed and punished by the teachers. Finally, the Johnsons took him out of school after an older nun told Bill that Louis was the 'worst type of native' and they placed him in a pre-apprenticeship welding course with the family company JLV Industries in the Perth suburb of Myaree. The Johnsons recall that, despite these setbacks, Louis still loved to socialise with white people, although he was quickly learning that many of them did not feel the same way about him.[24]

Like many other Aboriginal children adopted into white families Louis' identity and birth family became matters of great importance and urgency to him at this time. Bill later wrote that Louis was 'crying out for information about the whereabouts and identity of his birth family'.

The result of the adoption and the results of the isolation that Louis suffered from his birth family led to a great deal of grief and strife and loneliness for Louis in his teenage years and resulted in his abusing alcohol and getting into trouble with the police and all the time striving to find his own family.

All he wanted at that time was to meet them, find out who he was, who they were, then come back to Perth with us, finish his schooling, his apprenticeship, those types of things, but he just needed to touch base with them. It was very, very important at that time, for him to do that. In fact it was absolutely crucial that he did that and the way he was treated by those [Northern Territory Department of Community Welfare] was nothing short of disgraceful.[25]

At their teenage son's request the family went to Alice Springs in 1987 to attempt to find his birth family. Not knowing what to expect, Louis would say in anticipation, 'heartbreak or happiness'. They sought information from the Northern Territory Department of Community Development to no avail. Strict privacy laws still prevented the handing over of identifying information about parties to adoptions. The Northern Territory government maintains that prior to 1994, 'adoption legislation in the Northern Territory did not allow the release of identifying information to any person regardless of their stake in the adoption process'.[26]

Bill and Pauline remain extremely angry and bitter towards the Northern Territory government and its officials who refused to give Louis access to his records and through these, the possibility of being reunited with his family. As Bill recalls:

They gave him no help, no assistance, all they said to him in Alice Springs was we can't give you any information, just go to Darwin and see if they can tell you anything. We said that we know that his family is here, we know that you've got the family files, we know that he has got brothers and sisters because that's what we were told when we were adopting him. We said we believe that it's essential that he meets them, that he contacts them in some way for his own development. He needed that. They just absolutely refused to give us that information. Just blind bureaucracy.[27]

In Darwin they met with even more obstruction and indifference. Officials there told Louis to 'come back in seven years time when you are twenty-one and we might be able to do something for you'.[28] The Johnsons' pain was only made worse when they were told, after Louis' death, that the Northern Territory government officials were at least legally permitted to have told them, in 1987, that Louis' mother was still alive.[29] Louis' brother Kevin points to a photograph of Louis standing by the Todd River taken during that trip and laments that he and Dawna were living so close by. Bill believes that knowledge of his kin was essential to Louis' development and, as it tragically turned out, his survival.

In the midst of his emotional turmoil Louis continued to work at his father's factory. He also completed several solo flights towards his pilot's license and took up painting. He displayed considerable artistic talent and, reflecting on his desire to link with his people, he painted fine images of Aboriginal spirituality and Dreaming themes. However, Louis was also getting deeper into trouble with the law.

Louis had been targeted by police routinely from the age of twelve when he first began to move around Perth without his parents. As a young Aboriginal man who was often alone and could not handle even small amounts of alcohol, he was particularly vulnerable to police harassment. Louis was regularly stopped by police when driving the company utility, and finally had to display a card on the dashboard authorising him to use it. He was even accosted by police in the family home and had to prove he belonged there by referring the officers to a family portrait. He was ambushed by police when walking down the road near his home and only released when, fortunately, one officer recognised him – he was not one of the car thieves they had been lying in wait for.

Bill and Pauline Johnson were acutely aware that Louis' Aboriginality had marked him out for anyone to accuse, harass, and deprive him of his liberty – police or otherwise – in the street, in shops, anywhere. They say his most vulnerable times were when he was on his own, out of sight of family and friends, and sometimes only momentarily. 'That's when it would happen. It's like children falling into backyard swimming pools. In the brief moments when they were not watched, suddenly they're in trouble or they're gone'.[30] While he had many friends, Louis did not go about in a group of young Indigenous people, a factor which Bill and Pauline believe meant he was more vulnerable to opportunistic abuse – whether on his own or with others, he stood out.

In 1991 Louis was sentenced to twelve months in gaol for a minor offence. The Johnsons appealed against this in the Supreme Court, which quashed the sentence, on the grounds that it was excessively severe and did not fit the crime, and placed Louis on probation. That year the young man was also convicted of insulting a police officer and was put on probation for twelve months with a community service order. This conviction was unofficially cleared on appeal the following year, but after Louis' death. The court found that he had been provoked by a 'highly improper, uncalled for and provocative remark' made by the police sergeant.[31] Despite such harassment, Louis was quick to acknowledge that the police were not all the same. The Johnsons recalled his story of the constable at Central Station who responded angrily after the sergeant-in-charge told Louis, 'You know what your problem is, you're black', and said to Louis, 'Listen, we're not all like that,' and gave him a cigarette.[32] In retrospect, the Johnsons believe, despite their vigilance and unconditional support for Louis, that without the personal experience of living as Aboriginal people, they could not impart to Louis the full repertoire of skills he needed to survive in a racist society – skills that would have been drummed into him from an early age in an Aboriginal family.[33]

Unsafe streets

There was in fact a law and order hysteria gripping Perth at the time. From 1990 Perth's news media became increasingly preoccupied with juvenile and youth crime, which was presented as escalating to crisis proportions. Much of the coverage focused on Aboriginal youth, often in a discriminatory way. Although non-Aboriginal youths were also involved, Aboriginality was the only ethnicity identified in reports. The controversial police practice of pursuing stolen vehicles at high speeds in built-up areas resulted in over a dozen fatalities between 1990 and 1992. These deaths, and the sensationalising of burglaries and violent assaults – which in themselves were not unusual for a city of this size – were fodder for an extraordinary public campaign for severe penalties, organised by the populist talkback radio program, the Sattler File, on Radio 6PR. This radio program had significant advertising sponsorship from firms marketing home, car and personal security devices, all businesses that had obvious interests – converging with Howard Sattler's ratings quest – in the perception of rampant crime. The program was the publicity machine for a demonstration of up to 30,000 at Parliament House on 20 August 1991 – the 'Rally for Justice' – organised to pressure the government to simply incarcerate young offenders, and at which Sattler spoke. This was a complete rejection of the recommendations of the RCIADIC report released only three months earlier. Moreover, politicians and journalists simply took for granted the claims that youth crime was indeed spiralling out of control, and either failed to counter them or actively contributed to the myth for their own diverse purposes. The Sattler campaign's objectives were achieved in early February 1992 when the state Labor government caved in and pushed through parliament what were then the harshest juvenile crime laws in the country. At the same time Assistant Police Commissioner, Frank Zanetti, instructed police officers to adopt pro-active policing by targeting Aboriginal youth and he talked of introducing a youth curfew. This drew fire from the Human Rights and Equal Opportunity Commission, which issued a 'challenge to official and unofficial policies contravening young people's human rights' in Western Australia.[1] Early in March the *West Australian* newspaper reported a 'series of interchanges' between Human Rights Commissioner, Brian Burdekin, and Zanetti and the then premier, Carmen Lawrence. Zanetti initially denied having issued the directive to police to 'harass young people who were on the street' while the Premier was reported as saying that she had 'seen no suggestion that they are doing it' (harassing offenders) despite a concurrent parliamentary inquiry that reported 'significant abuses of power by police against young people'.[2]

Subsequent research has shown that in the peak year of the crime hysteria, 1991, juvenile and youth crime rates did not increase and possibly even *declined*. What did increase were public claims of increasing crime from demagogic media commentators such as Sattler, drum-beating politicians and police.[3] It was certainly the case that youth crime was a serious problem, but it had been for some time. Indigenous people had voiced their concerns about the problem and called for a range of solutions. The point here is that once the atmosphere of civil emergency took hold, so did demands for a single 'solution' – lock them up and throw away the key. This campaign relentlessly undermined public acceptance of progressive reforms in the areas of juvenile justice and Indigenous rights and welfare in this period. Instead the campaign fostered wide support for harsher punitive measures and increased public hostility to Indigenous rights and indifference to their circumstances. It worked to create a noxious public air of fear and malevolence toward Aboriginal youth in particular, of the kind conducive to racist thuggery and vigilantism, as Louis was to experience. Bill says:

> The amount of hysteria and hype and racism that was generated, particularly by people like Howard Sattler on the 6PR show created, I believe, the environment within which it was very easy for a couple of white people to murder Louis. If you cast your mind back to the 'Rally for Justice' outside Parliament House where fifteen or twenty thousand people

were screaming for the death penalty to be brought back, there were actual photographs and effigies of Hal Jackson [magistrate] from the Children's Court being strung up.[4]

According to Bill the public atmosphere was so bad that Louis, who was not interested in following current affairs, told him in late 1991:

'Dad, it's just not safe to be out on the streets any more'. This is after he had been assaulted in Northbridge while sitting outside a café drinking with a couple of white girls, and he was assaulted because an Aboriginal kid, a black kid, has no right to be talking to white girls.[5]

Murder

Around this time Louis made plans to return to Alice Springs to resume the search for his family. He would not, however, see his birthplace again. Only weeks after the attack in Northbridge Louis was brutally murdered by a different group of white youths.[1] At about three o'clock on the morning of 4 January 1992, his nineteenth birthday, Louis was walking home from a party in the affluent Perth suburb of North Beach. From the sequence of events established in court and in a coronial inquiry, it appears that he stopped to rest on the grass verge in North Beach Road, his legs protruding on to the road. Louis was seen by five white youths, three males and two females, passing by in a car. The two females and one of the males got out of the car further down the road, after which twenty-one-year-old Mark Wilder and the other male, who was seventeen,[2] returned in the car to watch from a short distance as another passing motorist, concerned for Louis' safety, stopped and moved the now sleeping young man fully on to the verge.[3] After this man had driven off, the killers made their move. Louis was bashed and Wilder pulled his legs back onto the road. Then, urged on by Wilder in the passenger seat with 'Do it, do it', the seventeen-year-old driver deliberately drove the car over Louis at high speed. The two then picked up the other three youths and returned with them to observe their victim, with the driver saying to the group, 'I got him, I am glad I got the black sod'. The killers and their friends sped off, leaving Louis for dead, with massive internal injuries including a shattered pelvis. A few hours later a passing cyclist came across him and called an ambulance. Before it arrived, Louis was still conscious enough to talk to the cyclist who, as a layperson, realised that Louis was seriously ill.

However, the ambulance attendants assumed, without making a proper examination, that Louis was not injured at all but had been sniffing petrol. They referred to him in casual and prejudicial terms to the cyclist. Instead of taking him to the hospital, they took him home, telling his younger sister that he was intoxicated, was not a hospital case, and should sleep it off in bed.[4] Bill and Pauline had left the house, for a business-related matter, before the ambulance arrived with Louis. Returning home around eight-thirty in the morning, and unaware of what had happened to him, they found Louis in bed and obviously ill. When the gravity of his condition became apparent, they called a second ambulance. His condition worsened and he lapsed into a coma just before the ambulance attendants arrived. His heart stopped while he was being carried on a stretcher to the ambulance.

In a taped confession to police after being arrested some days later the driver of the car admitted the racist motivation of his actions – 'because he was black'. He pleaded guilty to murder and was sentenced to seven years and nine months in prison. Wilder, who had described his victim as 'the black bastard', pleaded not guilty to the charge of murder, but was found guilty and given a mandatory life sentence in September 1992. The other youths involved were not charged with any offences.

The Johnsons have come to further conclusions about the degree of premeditation and ideological motivation of the murderers, based on what Louis was able to tell them while he was still conscious and on other subsequent evidence. Before he slipped into the coma Louis had managed to tell Pauline that he had been attacked by 'Nazis'. Louis told her, 'He hit me so hard'.[5] Bill and Pauline therefore believe Louis saw and heard his attackers and was beaten up by one or more of the group – before or after the other motorist stopped, attended to him and departed – after which the killers drove the car over him. Moreover, his attackers gave him an impression of a particular brand of racist thug. The Johnsons are not convinced that the other three youths did not take more direct roles in the killing.

In a press article Bill is quoted regarding the affluent social background of the killers, and the global racist elements involved:

Louis died because there were five kids in a car, one of whom admitted he was a member of National Action [a British fascist organisation]. He thought they could go out on a hunting party – like the pastoralists did many years ago in the Pilbara. These kids went to beat up or to kill a black person. Louis was the one that they met and killed. That's admitted. And we're not talking about deprived white kids who have a lack of education. One of the two girls in the car went to one of the most expensive schools in Perth. You're talking about the mortgage-belt in the northern suburbs where this murder occurred, committed by middle-class kids. The other obscenity which really hurts me is that none of the kids had been in this country longer than November 1988. They're all English.[6]

Here was a deadly confluence of British fascism and Australian racism.

The Coroner's report on the murder concluded that in their treatment of Louis the ambulance attendants had failed to follow a number of basic protocols, including failure to carry out a proper examination which would have detected Louis' major injuries. Coroner David McCann found that the operation of prejudicial stereotypes about Aboriginal people was indicated in the attendants' verbal communications with Louis and witnesses, and in written comments in the patient's records. The Coroner found that Louis had not been sniffing petrol and that the attendants had no reason to assume otherwise. The Coroner found that racial prejudice was a likely factor here.

> While witnesses have given evidence that the fact that Louis was of Aboriginal descent did not influence their decisions, the fact remains that within the general community there

are prejudices against persons of Aboriginal descent. These prejudices manifest themselves in many ways. Some are seen in instances of personal abuse while some are expressed in physical attacks causing injury as revealed in the Supreme Court proceedings which arose as a result of Louis' death. The use of derogatory terms when referring to persons of Aboriginal descent is common in the workplace and in the privacy of homes. It would be difficult in the light of the present widespread attitude to persons of Aboriginal descent, to conclude that there were not at least some unconscious prejudices in the decision-making process.[7]

The Johnsons took legal action against the ambulance officers and the St John Ambulance Association for their failure to treat Louis properly and thereby contributing to his death. The case was eventually settled out of court on the basis of an agreement that the ambulance service deposit $25,000 into a trust established for the Braedon family, and that it institute improved training of officers and employment screening procedures to ensure that the negligence and prejudice accorded to Louis would not be repeated.

Even after his death, after the seemingly closing act of racial prejudice against him by the ambulance attendants, Louis was to suffer final posthumous discrimination. Although the Perth media had been preoccupied with youth and juvenile crime – had given incidents of car theft, assaults and robberies headline and lead story status – its treatment of Louis' vicious murder by a group of youths was subdued. It was not taken up as an instance of the alleged spiralling youth crime wave. Nor did media and public commentators express outrage on

Louis' behalf, as a victim of crime, as they had for people assaulted and robbed or maimed and killed during police chases. His brutal murder was treated as a different kind of crime; one that failed to fit the actual, though unwritten, news agenda of innocent non-Aboriginal victims of Aboriginal lawlessness. The Sattler File's lack of interest in the killing was particularly conspicuous and revealing. Here was a cowardly and unprovoked attack on a citizen by a group of youths and juveniles, seemingly tailor-made for the Sattler theme of uncontrolled 'feral' teenagers roaming the streets. The relative lack of media interest in the murder of Louis Johnson in the days and weeks after it occurred raised serious questions about the entire structure of news reporting in Perth, and about the role of the media in shaping public attitudes towards crime, Aboriginality and justice. It demonstrated the media's racial selectivity in marshalling public sympathy for victims of crime, its professional, journalistic incompetence in failing to test assertions and impressions against fact, and its failure to pay regard to the social consequences of sensationalism. It was only after the *Sunday Times* ran a front page story and feature on the killing in March 1992, and through the efforts of Bill and Pauline Johnson to make the public aware of its significance, that other mainstream media began to show more than a cursorily routine interest.[8] Later that year a feature in the *Australian Magazine*[9] and a television current affairs report finally drew out the significance of Louis' case that the majority of the local mainstream media had largely neglected.[10]

Vowing not to bury their beloved adopted son until they had fulfilled their promise to reunite him with his birth family, the grief-stricken Johnsons and friends took his body back to Alice Springs.

> We lodged it [the coffin] at a funeral parlour, and then began knocking on doors. This time we were very, very angry; we'd been polite before and followed the rules, and it had got us nowhere.[11]

Within hours a receptionist at the Central Australian Aboriginal Child Care Agency (ACCA) saw in Louis' photograph his resemblance to a local woman. ACCA worker Brian White conveyed to the Northern Territory Department of Community Development Bill Johnson's threat that 'unless they cooperated we'd call in the national media and hold a press conference over Louis' dead body'.[12] Fifteen minutes later the Department rang back with the information that Louis' mother, brother and ninety-year-old grandfather were living in Alice Springs. The following day many of Louis' relatives met the Johnsons at the ACCA office. Louis' brother Kevin recalled the day. He was at first under the impression he was going to meet his long lost brother:

> Brian [White] had to come round pick me up and tell me to come and meet up with Bill and Pauline and we went into this ACCA. Sitting there, waiting there, I thought he was still alive you know. They told me he got killed. I thought I was coming to meet him.[13]

Louis was buried at Alice Springs cemetery on 20 January 1992. Over a hundred of his relatives attended the funeral, including his invalid mother Dawna. This caused Bill to wonder why the Department could not have arranged for Louis to be left in the care of an obviously large and caring family back in 1973. Pauline Johnson says of her experience:

> I personally felt ashamed because I had returned Louis to his own people dead. They had waited years for their son to come back. How can you look a hundred relatives in the face and say, 'I've got five photo albums to show you of your son?'[14]

Four months later on 3 June 1992, in the landmark Mabo decision, the Australian High Court recognised the existence of Native Title to Aboriginal lands. Before the year was out, on 10 December 1992, then Prime Minister Paul Keating acknowledged the culpabilities of non-Aboriginal Australia in a public speech in the inner-Sydney suburb of Redfern to mark the Year for the World's Indigenous People:

> We took the traditional lands and smashed the
>   traditional way of life.
> We brought the diseases. The alcohol.
> We committed the murders.
> We took the children from their mothers.
> We practised discrimination and exclusion.
> It was our ignorance and our prejudice.
> And our failure to imagine these things being done
>   to us.[15]

The Johnsons have maintained a relationship with the Braedons after Louis' death, visiting them in Alice Springs, and Kevin has stayed with the Johnson family in Perth. At the original time of writing in 1999 Kevin was still waiting to be reunited with his other missing siblings as, together with the Johnsons, he continued to fight the red tape preventing him from learning their identities.

Afterword

Aboriginal children living with white families or in institutions grow up outside this family-based 'safety zone'. They may have been fortunate – like Louis Johnson – to experience deep love from their adoptive families and the benefits of a comfortable life and educational opportunities that are out of the reach of most Aboriginal families, but they do not experience the deep emotional bonds that come from growing up within this wide circle of family. They do not become part of the kaleidoscope of events that binds family members together and that builds up living family histories over the years. Nor do they learn who they truly are by knowing how they fit into Aboriginal society and culture. Many grow up feeling alienated from white *and* black Australians and, as adults, spend years trying to locate their Aboriginal families and then struggling to learn how to fit in with their way of life.[1] It is a sobering fact of life that the experience of growing up in an Aboriginal family also acts as a form of 'life insurance' for young people living in a racist society. Drawing on a wealth of experiences, Aboriginal families teach their children how to survive racism – how to feel strong about their Aboriginal identity in the face of racist taunts and slurs, and teaching them that there are whole networks of relatives who will unconditionally back them up if trouble breaks out. Children learn the 'numbers game' at an early age – the importance in a potentially hostile world of moving within the 'safety zone' of groups of relatives who can protect them from harm. The tragic murder of Louis Johnson bears out the significance of this survival strategy. Louis Johnson, walking home alone from a party late at night was murdered. This terrible outcome and the interventions that shaped Louis' short life cannot be forgotten. They must be remembered in our hearts. At the same time we must act to ensure that such tragedies never happen again.

Additional study materials

The authors recommend the following further reading, listening and viewing:

Books and report

Bringing Them Home: A Report of the National Inquiry Into the Separation of Aboriginal and Torres Strait Islander Children From Their Families, Commonwealth Government, Human Rights and Equal Opportunity Commission, Sydney, 1997, at <http://www.humanrights.gov.au/publications/bringing-them-home-stolen-children-report-1997>.

Broken Circles: Fragmenting Indigenous Families 1800–2000, Haebich, A, Fremantle Arts Centre Press, Fremantle, 2000, at <http://www.fremantlepress.com.au/books/eBooks/1267?keywords=Broken%20Circles&x=8&y=13>.

Gambling on the First Race: A Comment on Racism and Talkback Radio — 6PR, the TAB and the Western Australian Government, Mickler, S, Centre for Research in Culture and Communication, Murdoch University, and the Louis St John Johnson Memorial Trust, Perth, 1992, at

<http://wwwmcc.murdoch.edu.au/ReadingRoom/CRCC/
gambling.html>.

Many Voices: Reflections on Experiences of Indigenous Child Separation,
Mellor, D & Haebich, A (eds), National Library of Australia,
Canberra, 2002.

The Myth of Privilege: Aboriginal Status, Media Visions, Public Ideas,
Mickler, S, Fremantle Arts Centre Press, Fremantle, 1998.

Songs and speech

'Lighthouse (*Song for Two Mothers*)', Archie Roach, from the album
Journey, Liberation Music, 2007. YouTube clip of Archie Roach
performing 'Lighthouse' prior to the screening of the film *Liyarn
Ngarn* at the National Museum of Australia on 22 January 2011 at
<http://www.youtube.com/watch?v=JYavLYTvtE8 >.

'Louis St John', Archie Roach, from the album *Looking for Butter Boy*,
Mushroom Records, 1997.

'The Redfern Address', Paul Keating, Redfern Park, Sydney, 10
December 1992. View transcript online at
<http://aso.gov.au/titles/spoken-word/keating-speech-redfern-
address/extras/>, YouTube clip at <https://www.youtube.com/
watch?feature=player_embedded&v=hhqAFLud228>.

Film and exhibition

Liyarn Ngarn, documentary film, directed by Martin Mhando, starring
Pete Postlethwaite, Archie Roach and Patrick Dodson, distributed
by ANTaR Incorporated, Sydney, 2007, at
<https://antar.org.au/shop/books-and-dvds-resources/liyarn-
ngarn>, YouTube film trailer at <http://www.youtube.com/
watch?v=ulT97q-crHI>.

'Separation', part of the *Eternity* exhibition, National Museum of
Australia, Canberra, 2013, at
<http://nma.gov.au/exhibitions/now_showing/eternity/
separation/>.

Notes

Abbreviations
AA (ACT)   Australian Archives (Australian Capital Territory)
AA (NT)   Australian Archives (Northern Territory)
NT WB AR   Northern Territory Welfare Branch Annual Report

Colonialism
1   Rowse, 1989.
2   Rowse, 1998a, p. 9.
3   Commonwealth Government, 1929, p. 7.
4   Rowse, 1998a.
5   This phrase has been widely used to refer to policies of Aboriginal protection in the early twentieth century.

Assimilation
1   Cited by Cummings, 1990, p. 39.
2   AA (NT) F1, 1952/250.
3   Harvey, 1946, p. 129.

4   Collmann, 1979, p. 384.
5   ibid., p. 389.
6   ibid.
7   Tatz, 1964, p. 16.
8   NT WB AR, 1968–69, p. 25.

Civil rights
1   Cummings, 1990, p. 129.

Equality in name only
1   *Centralian Advocate* (Alice Springs), 4.4.1974, p. 1.
2   *Centralian Advocate* (Alice Springs), 1.1.1973, p. 3.
3   ibid., p. 1.
4   *Centralian Advocate* (Alice Springs), 29.3.1973, p. 8; 12.4.1973, p. 6; 12.4.1973, p. 8.
5   *Centralian Advocate* (Alice Springs), 19.7.1973, p. 1.
6   *Centralian Advocate* (Alice Springs), 25.10.1973, p. 7.
7   *Centralian Advocate* (Alice Springs), 6.12.1973, p. 8.
8   Collmann, 1988, pp. 72–3.
9   Cutter, 1976, p. 6.
10 Heppell and Wigley, 1981, p. 128.
11 Shaw, 1977, pp. 12–13.
12 *Centralian Advocate* (Alice Springs), 16.4.1970, p. 8.
13 *Centralian Advocate* (Alice Springs), 25.5.1972, p. 1.
14 *Centralian Advocate* (Alice Springs), 16.8.1973, p. 12.
15 Faine, 1993, p. 68.
16 See *Centralian Advocate* (Alice Springs), 10.10.1974 to 6.2.1975.
17 *Age* (Melbourne), 18.11.1969.
18 *Centralian Advocate* (Alice Springs), 12.2.1970, p. 3.
19 Thornton, 1980, p. 2.
20 *Centralian Advocate* (Alice Springs), 19.2.1970, p. 11.
21 *Centralian Advocate* (Alice Springs), 12.2.1970, p. 3; 19.2.1970, p. 11.
22 *Centralian Advocate* (Alice Springs), 1.1.1973, p. 1. One possible effect of threats like the federal minister's was that officials involved in

child welfare could have felt themselves under increased pressure to remove babies from their mothers. Reprimanding public servants may have looked like concerted government action to some readers, but it could also simply be the minister scapegoating local public servants.

Self-determination and backlash

1 Faine, 1993, p. 30.
2 Collmann, 1988, p. 56.
3 ibid., p. 70.
4 Faine, 1993, p. 95.
5 ibid., pp. 70–1.
6 AA (NT) F1, 1968/3320, 5.5.1965.
7 AA (NT) F1, 1968/3320, 17.8.1966.
8 ibid.
9 AA (NT) F1, 1968/3320, 21.5.1969.
10 ibid.
11 ibid.
12 ibid.

The Braedon family

1 Kevin Braedon to Bill Johnson, 6.1.2000.
2 Cited in Donovan, 1988, p. 29.
3 ibid.
4 Born 1909, died c.1992.
5 Born c.1914, deceased.
6 Dorothy, deceased; Dawna, born 1944; Valerie, deceased; Raylene, deceased; Ernest, deceased; Eric, born 1959.
7 Eric Braedon interviewed by Anna Haebich at Little Sisters Camp, Alice Springs, March 1996.
8 Mary Williams interviewed by Anna Haebich at Little Sisters Camp, Alice Springs, March 1996.
9 Eric Braedon to Bill Johnson, 6.1.2000.
10 Tim Rowse personal communication, 1996.

11 Kevin Braedon interviewed by Anna Haebich at Alice Springs, August 1995.

12 Interviewed by Anna Haebich, March 1996.

13 Eric Braedon interviewed by Anna Haebich at Alice Springs, August 1995.

14 Kevin, born 1961; Vincent, deceased 1988; Ricky, born 1967; Jaclyn, born 1969.

15 Kevin Braedon interviewed by Anna Haebich at Alice Springs, August 1995.

16 Despite requests at the time by Kevin Braedon the Northern Territory Government did not release information to enable him to trace the whereabouts of these two siblings. Kevin believes he saw Jaclyn working as a nurse at an alcohol rehabilitation home in New South Wales.

17 Kevin Braedon interviewed by Anna Haebich at Alice Springs, August 1995.

18 ibid.

19 ibid.

20 ibid.

21 ibid.

Removal

1 Private correspondence between solicitors Ward and Keller and Bill and Pauline Johnson, 2.5.1974.

2 ibid.

3 The process of having a child declared a 'State child' involved the following steps. A welfare officer could take a child suspected to be 'destitute, neglected, incorrigible or uncontrollable' into custody without warrant and place him or her in an institution or with a 'responsible person.' Within fourteen days this officer was to make application to the Children's Court to have the child declared one of the above. The officer was obliged to 'take all steps' to ensure the child's parents' presence at the hearing of the application. Having declared the child any of the above, the options available to the

court were to commit the child to: the care of the Director of Child Welfare; to a person approved by the court; to an institution – until the age of eighteen or otherwise as specified – or to release the child on probation on conditions set by the court. Among the twelve possible definitions of 'neglected child' the following is likely to have been applied in Warren's case: a child who is not provided with necessary food, clothing, lodging, medical aid or nursing; or is neglected, ill-treated or exposed by his parents (*Child Welfare Ordinance 1958*).

4   Kevin Braedon interviewed by Anna Haebich at Alice Springs, August 1995.

5   Mary Williams interviewed by Anna Haebich at Little Sisters Camp, Alice Springs, March 1996.

Adoption

1   Private correspondence between solicitors Ward and Keller and Bill and Pauline Johnson, 2.5.1974. The Ordinance stipulated the grounds for dispensing with a parent or guardian's consent as: 'after reasonable inquiry that person could not be found; the person was in such a physical or mental condition as not to be capable of properly considering the question that he [sic] should give his consent; that a person has abandoned, deserted or persistently neglected or ill-treated the child; the person has, for a period of no less than one year, failed, without reasonable cause, to discharge the obligations of a parent or guardian, as the case may be, of the child; or, there are any other special circumstances by reason of which the consent may properly be dispensed with' (*Adoption Ordinance 1964*).

2   See for example, *Age* (Melbourne), 28.5.1957; AA (ACT) A884 A650 Part 1.

3   For instance, in New South Wales two decades later, only three of twenty-one Aboriginal children placed for adoption were adopted by Aboriginal families (Commonwealth Government, Australian Law Reform Commission, 1986, p. 234.) This was attributed to the

scarcity of Aboriginal families approved to adopt.

4   The Director of Child Welfare reported to the Court on applicants'
suitability to adopt on the following grounds. Applicants were
to be 'of good repute and ... fit and proper persons to fulfil the
responsibilities of parents of a child; ... suitable persons to adopt
the child having regard to all relevant matters including the age,
physical appearance, state of health, education (if any) and religious
upbringing or convictions (if any) of the child and the applicants,
and any wishes that may have been expressed by a parent or
guardian of the child ... with respect to the religious upbringing
of the child; and the welfare and interest of the child will be
promoted by the adoption' (*Adoption Ordinance 1964*).

5   Refer to chapter 8 in *Broken Circles* by Anna Haebich.

6   Northern Territory Government, 1996, p. 13. The Report of the
Martin Inquiry into welfare was tabled in the Northern Territory
Legislative Assembly in 1979. This signalled the beginning of a
period of legislative and administrative review and reform which
continued during the 1980s in the areas of family and children's
services in the Northern Territory.

7   This Act was strongly influenced by the United States' *Indian Child
Welfare Act 1978* (Commonwealth Government, Australian Law
Reform Commission, 1986, p. 250.).

8   The Matter of F (an infant) McMillen v Larcombe, cited
in Commonwealth Government, Australian Law Reform
Commission, 1986, p. 239; McCorquodale, 1987, pp. 271–4.

9   Commonwealth Government, Australian Law Reform
Commission, 1986, p. 239.

10   McCorquodale, 1987, p. 272.

11   ibid., p. 273.

12   Faine, 1993, p. 131.

The Johnsons

1   Submission by William Johnson to the Human Rights and Equal
Opportunity Commission, National Inquiry into the Separation of

Aboriginal and Torres Strait Islander Children from their Families, 1996, transcribed from audiotape.

2   Bill and Pauline Johnson to Anna Haebich and Steve Mickler, Perth, 20.1.2000.

3   Submission by William Johnson to the Human Rights and Equal Opportunity Commission, National Inquiry into the Separation of Aboriginal and Torres Strait Islander Children from their Families, 1996, transcribed from audiotape.

4   Bill and Pauline Johnson to Anna Haebich and Steve Mickler, Perth, 20.1.2000.

5   Submission by William Johnson to the Human Rights and Equal Opportunity Commission, National Inquiry into the Separation of Aboriginal and Torres Strait Islander Children from their Families, 1996, transcribed from audiotape.

6   ibid.

7   This heartless scenario was not uncommon in Aboriginal adoptions of this period in the Northern Territory.

8   Private correspondence between solicitors Ward and Keller and Bill and Pauline Johnson, 27.8.1974.

Perth

1   Commonwealth Government, Department of Aboriginal Affairs, 1984, p. 138.

2   Commonwealth Government, Human Rights and Equal Opportunity Commission, 1989, p. 40.

3   Commonwealth Government, Royal Commission into Aboriginal Deaths in Custody, 1991, p. 258; Commonwealth Government, Equal Opportunity Commission, 1989, p. 40.

4   Commonwealth Government, Department of Aboriginal Affairs, 1984, p. 131.

5   ibid., p. 115.

6   Commonwealth Government, Australian Law Reform Commission, 1986, p. 236.

7   Commonwealth Government, Department of Aboriginal Affairs,

1985, p. 39.

8   Collard and Palmer, 1991, p. 86.

9   Commonwealth Government, Royal Commission into Aboriginal Deaths in Custody, 1991, p. 571.

10 Commonwealth Government, Department of Aboriginal Affairs, 1984, p. 114.

11 Australian National Opinion Poll Market Research, 1985, p. 13.

12 ibid., p. 58.

13 ibid., p. 52.

14 ibid., p. 57.

15 'Noongar' is the term used by Aboriginal people in the south-west of Western Australia to refer to themselves. This word has various spellings; this usage follows that used by the South West Aboriginal Land and Sea Council.

16 Collard and Palmer, 1991, p. 85.

17 Western Australian Government, 1984, p. 28.

18 Collard and Palmer, 1991.

19 Cited in Commonwealth Government, Royal Commission into Aboriginal Deaths in Custody, 1991, pp. 401–2.

20 Submission by William Johnson to the National Inquiry into the Separation of Aboriginal and Torres Strait Islander Children from their Families, 1996, transcribed from audiotape.

21 Pauline Johnson interviewed by Anna Haebich at Wattle Grove, Western Australia, October 1995; Bill and Pauline Johnson to Anna Haebich and Steve Mickler, Perth, 20.1.2000.

22 Submission by William Johnson to the National Inquiry into the Separation of Aboriginal and Torres Strait Islander Children from their Families, 1996, transcribed from audiotape.

23 ibid; Bill and Pauline Johnson to Anna Haebich and Steve Mickler, Perth, 20.1.2000.

24 Pauline Johnson interviewed by Anna Haebich at Wattle Grove, Western Australia, October 1995.

25 Submission by William Johnson to the National Inquiry into the Separation of Aboriginal and Torres Strait Islander Children from

their Families, 1996, transcribed from audiotape.

26 Northern Territory Government, 1996, p. 31. The *Adoption of Children Act 1994* provides parties to adoption with access to identifying information. The Act endeavoured to balance the need to 'remove secrecy from the process of adoption' and at the same time to 'honour past guarantees of confidentiality'. In respect to adoptions prior to 1994, the release of information to an adoptee over sixteen years of age can apply at any time. Adoptees under sixteen must have their adoptive parents' consent. Relinquishing parents can only apply for information which identifies the adoptee after he or she reaches eighteen. Adoptive parents can only obtain information which does not identify relinquishing parents. Any party, with the exception of the adoptive parents, can lodge a veto on releasing identifying information. (ibid., 1996, pp. 49–50.)

27 Submission by William Johnson to the National Inquiry into the Separation of Aboriginal and Torres Strait Islander Children from their Families, 1996, transcribed from audiotape.

28 ibid.

29 ibid.

30 Bill and Pauline Johnson to Anna Haebich and Steve Mickler, Perth, 20.1.2000.

31 Supreme Court of Western Australia, 1993, pp. 359–365.

32 Bill and Pauline Johnson to Anna Haebich and Steve Mickler, Perth, 20.1.2000.

33 ibid.

Unsafe streets

1 Sercombe, 1997, p. 52.

2 *West Australian*, 7.3.1992; Sercombe, 1997, p. 52.

3 Mickler and McHoul, 1997.

4 Submission by William Johnson to the National Inquiry into the Separation of Aboriginal and Torres Strait Islander Children from their Families, 1996, transcribed from audiotape.

5 ibid.

Murder

1 This reconstruction of events by Steve Mickler sources Johnson, 1996, and McCann, 1994. See also Mickler, 1998, pp. 69–74.

2 As a juvenile at the time, he cannot be named under Western Australian law.

3 As a juvenile at the time, he cannot be named under Western Australian law.

4 In a tragic irony, Louis' middle name was St John, and he was a fully paid-up subscriber to the St John's Ambulance Fund.

5 McCann, 1994, p. 20; Bill and Pauline Johnson to Anna Haebich and Steve Mickler, Perth, 20.1.2000.

6 *Militant*, April 1992.

7 McCann, 1994, p. 31.

8 Saxon, 1992, p. 1, p. 9.

9 Laurie, 1992, pp. 16–20, p. 45.

10 Notable exceptions to this were a moving award-winning radio feature story, Louis Johnson, by Adrian Shaw and Nellie Green aired on Perth Aboriginal Radio 6AR in 1992, and serious coverage in various human rights, union and left-wing papers.

11 Laurie, 1992, pp. 16–20, p. 45.

12 ibid.

13 Kevin Braedon interviewed by Anna Haebich at Alice Springs, August 1995.

14 Laurie, 1992, pp. 16–20, p. 45.

15 Extracted from 'The Redfern Address' made by Paul Keating on 10 December 1992 at Redfern Park, Sydney.

Afterword

1 See Read and Edwards, 1989; Commonwealth Government, Human Rights and Equal Opportunity Commission, 1997; Link-Up (New South Wales) Aboriginal Corporation and Wilson, 1997; Read, 1999.

Bibliography

Books and reports

Australian National Opinion Poll Market Research, *Land Rights. Winning Middle Australia: An Attitude and Communications Research Study. Presented to the Department of Aboriginal Affairs January 1985*, ANOP Market Research for Government and Industry, Crows Nest, New South Wales, 1985.

Collard, L. and Palmer, D., 'Aboriginal Young People in the Southwest of Western Australia: Implications for Youth Policy', in White, R. and Wilson, B. (eds), *For Your Own Good: Young People and State Intervention in Australia. Special edition of Journal of Australian Studies*, La Trobe University Press, Bundoora, Victoria, 15 (31), 1991, pp. 78–83.

Collmann, J., 'Women, Children, and the Significance of the Domestic Group to Urban Aborigines in Central Australia', *Ethnology*, 18 (4), 1979, pp. 379–397.

Collmann, J., *Fringe-dwellers and Welfare. The Aboriginal Response to Bureaucracy*, University of Queensland Press, St Lucia, 1988.

Commonwealth Government, Bleakley, J, *The Aboriginals and*

Half-Castes of Central Australia and North Australia, Government
Printer, Canberra, 1929.

Commonwealth Government, Department of Aboriginal Affairs,
Aboriginal Social Indicators 1984, Australian Government Publishing
Service, Canberra, 1984.

Commonwealth Government, Department of Aboriginal Affairs.
Aboriginal Statistics 1985, Australian Government Publishing Service,
Canberra, 1985.

Commonwealth Government, Australian Law Reform Commission.
The Recognition of Aboriginal Customary Laws, Volume 1, Australian
Government Publishing Service, Canberra 1986.

Commonwealth Government, Human Rights and Equal Opportunity
Commission, *Our Homeless Children: Report of the National Inquiry
Into Homeless Children*, Australian Government Publishing Service,
Canberra, 1989.

Commonwealth Government, Royal Commission into Aboriginal
Deaths in Custody, Commissioner P. L. Dodson, *Regional Report
of Inquiry into Individual Deaths in Custody in Western Australia of the
Royal Commission into Aboriginal Deaths in Custody*, Vol. 1, Australian
Government Publishing Service, Canberra, 1991.

Cummings, B., *Take This Child. From Kahlin Compound to the Retta
Dixon Children's Home*, Aboriginal Studies Press, Canberra, 1990.

Cutter, T. N., *Report on Alice Springs Fringe Camps*, Central Australian
Aboriginal Congress, Alice Springs, 1976.

Donovan, P., *Alice Springs: Its History and the People Who Made It*, Alice
Springs Town Council, Alice Springs, 1988.

Faine, J., *Lawyers in Alice. Aboriginal and Whitefella's Law*. Federation
Press, Annandale, Sydney, 1993.

Harvey, A., 'Ethnic and Sociological Study of an Australian Mixed
Blood Group in Alice Springs, Northern Territory with Reference
to Ethnic Assimilation and Interaction of Groups', *Elkin Papers*,
University of Sydney, 1946.

Heppell, M. and Wigley, J., *Black Out in Alice. A History of the
Establishment and Development of Town Camps in Alice Springs*,

Monograph no. 26, Developmental Studies Centre, Australian National University, Canberra, 1981.

Laurie, V., 'Victims, Crime and Prejudice in the West', *Australian Magazine*, 7.11.1992, pp. 16–20, p. 45.

Link-Up (New South Wales) Aboriginal Corporation and Wilson, T. J., *In the Best Interests of the Child? Stolen Children: Aboriginal Pain, White Shame*. Aboriginal History Incorporated, Canberra, 1997.

McCann, D., 'Inquest into the Death of Louis St John Johnson, 18.3.1994', Typescript, Perth Coroners Office, 1994.

McCorquodale, J., *Aborigines and the Law: A Digest*, Aboriginal Studies Press, Canberra, 1987.

Mickler, S., *The Myth of Privilege*, Fremantle Arts Centre Press, Fremantle, 1998.

Mickler, S. and McHoul, A., 'Sourcing the Wave: Crime Reporting, Aboriginal Youth and the Perth Press', *Media International Australia*, 86, 1998, pp. 122–52.

Northern Territory Government, 'National Inquiry into the Separation of Aboriginal and Torres Strait Islander Children from their Families: Northern Territory Government Interim Submission', Darwin, Typescript, Human Rights and Equal Opportunity Commission, Sydney, 1996.

Read, P., *A Rape of the Soul So Profound: The Return of the Stolen Generations*, Allen & Unwin, Sydney, 1999.

Read, P. and Edwards, C. (eds), *The Lost Children: Thirteen Aboriginal Accounts of Northern Territory History*. Institute for Aboriginal Development, Alice Springs, 1989.

Rowse, T., 'White Flour, White Power? Colonial Authority, Rationing and the Family in Alice Springs', PhD Thesis, University of Sydney, 1989.

Rowse, T., *White Flour, White Power. From Rations to Citizenship in Central Australia*, Cambridge University Press, Cambridge, 1998.

Saxon, M., 'Car Killing No Treatment', 'Long-lost Murdered Teenager Got "Home" Too Late', *Sunday Times* (Perth), 8.3.1992.

Sercombe, H., 'Youth Crime and the Economy of News Production', in Bessant, J. and Hill, R. (eds), *Youth Crime and the Media*, National Clearing House for Youth Studies, Hobart, 1997, pp. 43–54.

Supreme Court of Western Australia, 'Johnson vs Lapham', *Western Australian Law Reports*, 6, 1993.

Thornton, F., 'Appendix 1, Situation Report: Aboriginal Communities in Alice Springs and Fringe Camps', 1979, reprinted in Bell, D. and Ditton, P. (eds), *Law: The Old and the New*, Aboriginal History for Central Australian Aboriginal Legal Aid Service, Canberra, 1980.

Tatz, C., 'Aboriginal Administration in the Northern Territory of Australia', PhD Thesis, Australian National University, Canberra, 1964.

Western Australian Government, Seaman, P., *The Aboriginal Land Inquiry Volume 1*. Government Printer, Perth, 1984.

Government records and reports

Australian Archives (Australian Capital Territory)

Australian Archives (Northern Territory)

Northern Territory Welfare Branch Annual Reports

Private papers

Correspondence between Ward and Keller and Mr and Mrs W Johnson.

Interviews and submissions

Kevin Braedon interviewed by Anna Haebich at Alice Springs, August 1995.

Eric Braedon and Mary Williams interviewed by Anna Haebich at Little Sisters Camp, Alice Springs, 16 March 1996.

Pauline Johnson interviewed by Anna Haebich at Wattle Grove, Western Australia, October 1995.

Submission by William Johnson to the Human Rights and Equal Opportunity Commission, National Inquiry into the Separation of Aboriginal and Torres Strait Islander Children from their Families, 1996.

Newspapers and magazines

Age (Melbourne)
Australian
Centralian Advocate (Alice Springs)
Militant
Sunday Times (Perth)
West Australian (Perth)

Academic journals

Ethnology
Journal of Australian Studies
Media International Australia

Song lyrics and speech

Keating, P., 'The Redfern Address', presented at Redfern Park, Redfern, New South Wales, 10 December 1992, at <http://aso.gov.au/titles/spoken-word/keating-speech-redfern-address/extras/>.

Roach, A., 'Louis St John', from the album *Looking for Butter Boy*, Mushroom Records, 1997, reproduced with permission of the artist and Mushroom Music Publishing, Albert Park, Victoria.

CPSIA information can be obtained at www.ICGtesting.com
Printed in the USA
BVOW11s1647280114

343238BV00003B/13/P